# Restoring the
# Power
# of Family

JONATHAN CLAUSSEN, MD

WESTBOW°
PRESS
A DIVISION OF THOMAS NELSON
& ZONDERVAN

Scripture taken from the New King James Version. Copyright 1979, 1980, 1982 by Thomas Nelson, inc. Used by permission. All rights reserved.

WestBow Press books may be ordered through booksellers or by contacting:

WestBow Press
A Division of Thomas Nelson & Zondervan
1663 Liberty Drive
Bloomington, IN 47403
www.westbowpress.com
1 (866) 928-1240

ISBN: 978-1-4908-5070-2 (sc)
ISBN: 978-1-4908-5069-6 (hc)
ISBN: 978-1-4908-5068-9 (e)

Library of Congress Control Number: 2014915809

Printed in the United States of America.

WestBow Press rev. date: 09/22/2014

# Contents

To my Abba Father.

Daddy God, thank You for Your unquenchable love for me. Thank You that You never stopped pursuing me and my heart.

Thank You that You trusted me with Your secrets.

I am a son of the Most High God. I am fully satisfied in Your embrace!

This book is *from* You … and this book is *for* You!

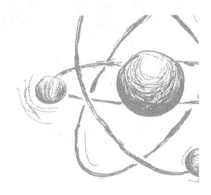

# Preface

I realize that I've been set up. Sometimes the Lord fills you in on His great plan for your life, step-by-step, and sometimes He doesn't. Sometimes there are outlines and perhaps even a ten-year plan, and sometimes things happen suddenly. When you're in the middle of just doing life, the ebbs and flows, the ups and downs, it is easy to lose the big picture. At the time of writing this book, I've been able to take a step back and look over the course of my last decades of life and indeed realize ... I've been set up.

I was raised in a wonderful Christian home in the suburbs of Minneapolis, Minnesota. My upbringing was not ravaged by abuse, neglect, pain, or hurt that is so often seen and experienced by American youth. I was a good Christian kid who truly loved the Lord. I never did drugs, never drank alcohol, was a good student, was not overly rebellious, and didn't swear or curse—not a very interesting or radical testimony. My father was a pastor, my mom a homemaker. I lived somewhat of an enchanted "storybook" childhood.

Even though having a father who was a pastor certainly had its difficulties, with a decent amount of expectation and teasing, there was a day that would turn out to be pivotal for the Claussen family. My pastor father had a radical encounter with the living God! My mom and dad were swept away in the extravagant love and transformational power of the Holy Spirit. This started our family on a pursuit for the authentic Christian experience. As a young boy, I did find this somewhat intimidating and, at times, embarrassing. However, it was authentic. This made an impression on a young boy's heart. Kids can sense "phony" a mile away. Gently, the Holy Spirit began to entice me into His presence, and I too began to have real, authentic encounters with my loving Father. The reality of a loving God was mine at an early age. The culture of His love was something I inherited from my parents, and the reality of it in my own life created a young man sold out to God.

I used to be self-conscious or ashamed at my somewhat dull and uninteresting testimony. As I have become more immersed into the issues of family, I now realize how truly radical and rare it is. There was a time when I would apologize or be somewhat sheepish about my solid upbringing, loving family environment, and godly heritage. Now I have learned to never apologize for that grace in my life. I'm truly thankful to my parents and to my siblings for the godly seed and effort they put forth into my life. When the Lord asked me to share His truths and His original intent for family, I didn't have to run that information through a filter of my pain. Because my life was not defined by pain, disillusionment, and destructive choices, I was able to simply study Scripture and listen to Daddy's voice clearly. I didn't feel the need to alter Scripture or offer any dilution so that my personal pain would be less. For that, I am grateful.

Furthermore, I grew up in a culture where family was fun. I always felt my dad truly enjoyed being with us, and my mom was a stay-at-home mom who invested her time and unwavering interest in our lives. When my mom asked, "How was school today?" it was never good enough to say, "Fine." It always required a sit-down chat with detailed stories and often laughter. Still, to this day, my mother makes people feel like they're the most important person in the world.

My parents created a strong family culture. This was well defined by honor, respect, and boundaries, with equal doses of games, fun, and laughter. My siblings are still some of my favorite people on the planet, and there have been times when we laughed so hard together we were sore the next day! Evidently, the importance and significance of family was branded into my life at an early age. The Lord told my father that he would "father a family movement," and I believe with all my heart that that this is just the beginning.

The Lord further set me up for this family movement on the day my eyes met the eyes of a gorgeous young lady at church. I quickly fell in love, and I have been falling more in love with her ever since. Amy's primary dream when growing up was to be a wife and a mother. While I was starting medical school, she was finishing nursing school. An instructor asked her in one of her nursing classes where she saw herself in five years, expecting a professional, clinical-type response. Instead, she said, "Hopefully retired from nursing, married, and raising children." Having also been raised in a godly, loving home, the value and desire for family was as strong in her as it was in me.

We attended a premarital class together through our church, and the counselors asked if we wanted to have children. Of course we enthusiastically said yes. Then, unexpectedly, they asked, "*Why* do you want to have children?" This is something that we actually had talked about, so we were easily able to explain to them that the call on our life was to have and raise children. They smiled and explained that we were the first couple in all of their counseling experience who articulated an answer to that question.

The call on our life was indeed to raise children, and boy, did God deliver! Our home is filled with the laughter and joy of our eight beautiful children. Once again, my life focused and concentrated on family. Raising children is not for the weakhearted; we have had our share of heartache and challenges. Any heartache, however, is swallowed up by joy and wonderment, as each child shares such a uniqueness of his or her life with us. Raising eight children certainly does not make us parenting experts. It does, however, give us more attempts at getting it right! As it was with my heart when I was a young boy, my wife and I have the pleasure of seeing the authentic love and worship in our children's lives for their heavenly Father. The authenticity afforded to us, as inheritance from our parents, has now been passed to our children but in a greater measure and normalcy than we experienced at that age. It is the demonstration of the power of inheritance.

My adventure into family continued when, in the summer of 2009, we began a ministry in our home with a collection of hungry believers, which we called the Glory Barn. This was created, very simply, to host the presence of the Lord and to allow freedom in worship. Amy and I would host, and our children would fully participate in extravagant worship; often, we were accompanied by both sets of our parents. It has demonstrated such a powerful and beautiful picture of family worship, and many have commented that it was this fact that drew them to the Glory Barn.

As I unexpectedly saw the power of family influence at the Glory Barn, the Lord began to speak to me regarding His design for family. While basking in the excitement that this new ministry brought to our home, He also began to work in my heart. Amy and I went through a very real and poignant season in our lives when we were instructed by the Holy Spirit to simplify, slow down, and focus on our family. It was a season of "hunkering down." We began to have more quiet talks as a family, and the Lord very specifically told me to prioritize playing games with my kids. As mentioned above, the culture of the Claussen home was never to shy away from a good board game, but this season was ramped up to an even greater level.

Even though I felt a calling in my life "for more," there was such a winnowing and paring down in my life that I was overwhelmed with the notion and satisfaction of simply being a husband and daddy. Despite this, the vision and revelation of the true impact and original purpose of family was downloading into my life. Notebook page after notebook page was filled with fresh insight and revelation. Yet instead of releasing it, I was content with simply living it.

One day, things began to shift. I had been so moved with the sincerity of the truth about my family and the seed that was being sown into my children that my heart began to stir in compassion for others. I felt so stirred in my spirit that now was the time to release it. I drove home that day, looked at my wife, and said, "We need to talk." She calmly responded, "I know." On the same day, at the same time, my wife began to feel the same stir. What had been packaged for us in such a real, organic way over the past season, with God's truth living out in our family, was now to be delivered to others. It was "go time."

Through the providence of a loving God, what initially brought contentment changed in one day. This revelation was a word for now, a word to be released, a word to offer hope and healing to families around the world. This was a word to empower families to be everything they were created to be and to receive the fullness of their identity and inheritance. This was the start of the Family Restoration Project. We would be a family releasing His truth about family.

Interestingly, before this crazy adventure began, I was called to be a physician. My specialty? You guessed it—family medicine. I told you I was set up! I chose family medicine simply because I liked it. No audible voice from God, no lightning bolt, no prophetic word—I chose it because I like people and the variety that family medicine offered. Little did I know that my practice would set an absolute foundation for what the Lord would have in mind decades later.

Finally, the Lord has filled me with passion for family that has been equal to my preparation. I am passionate for *your* family. Your family is so much bigger and more powerful than you can even imagine. Whether your family experience is of the "storybook" variety or one of pain and despair, my hope is that this book and our ministry can bring revelation of what the Father originally intended for family, so that it can provide healing where it is needed, inspiration, and propulsion to every family to be all it was created to be.

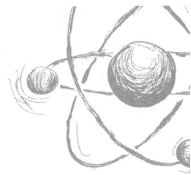

# Acknowledgments

To my beloved wife, Amy: this book is as much yours as it is mine. You are my "one flesh," and all that I have is yours. Thank you for never doubting that this could be done and providing the time to make it happen. You have always believed in my wildest dreams, and my love for you is beyond measure.

To Jacob, Emma, Benjamin, Lydia, Maggie, Elijah, Silas, and Sadie: thank you for believing in me and cheering me on. I couldn't be more proud to be your daddy, and I love you so much. I am very grateful that you are embracing the destiny that is upon our family. We've only just begun!

To my parents, Don and Heather, and Amy's parents, Larry and Wilma: so much of this book is built upon the foundation that you have laid for our family. Thank you for paying the price and for your unconditional support and love toward me.

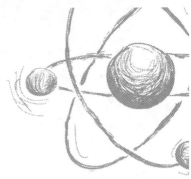

# Introduction

At the time of writing this book, I am practicing family medicine full time in a small rural community in central Minnesota. I offer full scope, small-town family medicine. On any given day, I practice pediatrics, obstetrics, and geriatrics and even take shifts as an emergency room physician. I take delight in where the Lord has placed me professionally; with caring, exceptional partners and a rewarding practice. I am most grateful, however, for being invited into the families of this small, charming community. To provide them care and compassion is truly an honor. And yes, as a small-town doctor, I have actually been paid with butchered chickens after an occasional house-call.

Because of this, I have a unique perspective on family. I'm often surprised at how willing people are to open up about their lives and family situations. Believe me, they tell me many more things that I care to know. This has exposed me to "the good, the bad, and the ugly" of family life.

I have seen big, burly farmers reduced to tears as they hold their newborn children. I've also seen new mothers more interested in how quickly they could be discharged from the hospital so they could smoke (or worse) than in their beautiful newborn babies. I've seen inspiring adoptions and heartless abandonments. I've seen families caring for their developmentally disabled children with such love and sacrifice, with very little offered in return, and I've seen abuses of every kind toward children that would make any heart weep. I've seen a husband serve sacrificially as the sole caregiver for his wife with Alzheimer's, even though she might not know who he is, and I've seen marriages crumble all around me, leaving a wake of devastation in their lives and in their children's lives. I've seen families gather around their loved one on their deathbeds, holding their hands, praying and singing over them, and recounting stories of honor and thankfulness for the life they shared, and I've seen the alcoholic, with body broken and weathered, dying all alone.

As a Christian, you can respond to this hurt and dysfunction in two different ways: you can lose hope, curl up in the fetal position, and wait for Jesus to return; or you can be moved by compassion, ask the Lord for strategy, and jump in with both feet. I've been tempted by the former, but I'm compelled by the latter. This book is written from the compassion and the passion in my heart for family. I feel strongly that Christian families need to be on the front lines—the leaders of this movement to bring restoration to the world. It is *not* hopeless. Is *not* hopeless for your family. It is *not* hopeless for our nation. It is *not* hopeless for our world.

I believe that the Lord has given me strategy, revelation, and truth that is in His heart for family. Scripture is the most compelling love story and reveals the undeniable truth that the Father's original intent was to use family as His means to display heaven on earth. The Father's plan is to bring healing to families and to raise up powerful and purposeful families to influence the earth. I hope when you are finished reading this book, I will have proven this to you.

When we reveal what is the Father's best, the Enemy often tries to bring condemnation and judgment. Truth is always intended to set us free, never to place us in bondage. Family is an incredibly emotional and vulnerable topic, and I will be asking you to go to some difficult and vulnerable places. This is because the very fabric of family is unraveling, and time is too short to "tap dance" around the issues of family. However, my heart and certainly the Father's heart are never to bring condemnation. None of us has done family perfectly, but now, more than ever, we need to aim for a target and always strive for His best. Charles Spurgeon said, "I have heard it said that if there is a crooked stick and you want to show how crooked it is, you need not waste words and description. Place a straight one by the side of it, and the thing is done directly."

This book is not intended to only inspire or provide motivational family counseling. This book won't contain ways to make your kids feel special, provide encouragement to go on dates with your wife, or deliver "the seven steps to a happy home." All of these things are important, but this book deals directly with the core—the root issues that affect family as a whole.

The term nuclear family is a sociological term describing a husband, a wife, and their children. It is appropriately named the nuclear family because this group of people forms the very nucleus of a home, but it also has been and always will be the very core and nucleus of society in general. This has been established since the beginning of time. Furthermore, I believe it is also appropriately named because the family is powerful; it is nuclear. Nuclear energy, when safe and contained, is one of the most effective and efficient forms of energy known on earth. However, when nuclear energy is uncontained, when there are cracks or malfunctions in the power plants, nuclear energy can have the most destructive and devastating effect on the earth. Could anything describe family more perfectly?

Because of our human nature, we try to minimize pain. For so long, because family has been such a source of pain and disillusionment for such a large percentage of people, we attempt to distance ourselves from that pain. The logical way to accomplish that goal would be through redefinition. If we change what family is and what family means, then maybe our disappointment and expectation would be less. If we are free from the commitment and the culture that is required to make family great, then maybe we can look elsewhere and surround ourselves with those who will love us and not hurt us. Then, if they do hurt us, we will have greater freedom to leave again and continue to look elsewhere. This creates a culture of temporary love, which only serves as an anesthetic to the real pain that can be satisfied only by our heavenly Father's love and through *real* family.

Everyone is on a quest for belonging. Everyone is trying to address the following questions: Who am I? Why am I here? To whom do I belong? Everyone is on a quest for family. I believe that this zealousness has created a culture where it seems as if everything is considered family. We call the people we work with family; our classmates are referred to as family; our closest friends are called family; and even the Olive Garden restaurant advertises, "When you're here, you're family." These people in our lives can offer us many things (like warm breadsticks) … but they cannot deliver family. It is my opinion that although church was intended to strengthen, equip, and empower families, it was *never* intended to be a substitute for family.

The result of everything being referred to as family is a dilution of the true meaning and purpose of the word. Because of the hurt in our own families, we desperately hope that these other relationships could indeed be family to us. The problem is, they can't. They simply can't be something that they were never created to be.

There is simply no other word like family. It is God-given and God-ordained. And whether you realize it or not, *your family carries great power.* It is time to flip the switch and let this truth settle deep within your spirit, so the very culture of your home can resonate with that power.

You will learn in this book that the Creator of all things set everything into motion, with family at the core of His plan. Sin and rebellion separated us from that plan, however, the loving Father sent Jesus on a restoration mission. We now can once again enter into the fullness of what He created our families to be.

You will receive core strategies that will bring healing to your life and your relationships. You will see how this healing creates a domino effect that will strengthen marriages, empower parents, bring freedom, and an inheritance mindset to our children, and then, in turn, change the culture of church and society as a whole.

Greater understanding of your inheritance will be provided. You will learn to receive all that was intended for your family and then pass this on to future generations as an inheritance.

This book will review and restore the command to subdue the earth. It will also explain what will happen when Christian families are secure in their identity and lead from a place of authority and influence.

If you want all that the Father intended for your family, for you, for your children, and for your children's children, then I ask that you lean into this book with all of your heart. Allow the God of restoration to do a work in you, and allow the God of restoration to do a work through you and through your family.

# Chapter 1: Let There Be Light

## The Father's Original Plan for Family

For something to be restored, you need to know two essential things. First, you need to know its inherent value. There would be little point in spending time, money, and effort on a project if the outcome would have no increase in value. Second, you would need to know what it originally looked like. Imagine a restoration project on an old boat or automobile. One of the first steps would be to find an old photo or drawing in order to know its original form or color.

So, with the restoration of family, the same two questions apply. What is the inherent value of family, and what did it originally look like? We need to go back and explore chapter 1 of Genesis, for it is there that we will find the inherent value and purpose of family from the very foundations of the earth. We will discover the highly dramatic moment when the creator God first addresses His creation, made in His image. Then, in chapter 2, we will find what family was originally intended to look like as it was fulfilling its purpose on the earth. We will see what a home looks like that is created by a loving Father in relationship with His beloved children.

# In the Beginning

Genesis 1 is the story of creation. It describes the six days of God's creative work, which concludes on the seventh day of rest. Genesis 1:1–2:3 is clearly a marked-off section and was intended to be a distinct narrative. It opens with the truth that God created both the heavens and the earth but then proceeds to focus on the earth. It then describes the Spirit poised for creative action, hovering over the waters. Then God said, "Let there be light," and there was light. The Bible is clear that this light is not from our sun. The sun was not created until day four. I find it fascinating and heartwarming that Scripture begins with the light of the presence of God and ends with the light of the presence of God (see Rev. 22:5). Creation continues with the separation of water with the creation of the firmament. He then gathered the waters so dry land could appear. The dry land was then filled with vegetation. Next, the stars, the sun, and the moon were created. He then began to populate the seas, land, and sky that were just formed. Finally, He formed the solitary man and woman of the human race, whom God made to look like Himself, and the human pair were given their orders and instructions. God's work was over; it was good, and on the seventh day He rested.

It is clear from Scripture that there is a concentration of importance on the sixth day. The first five days of creation set the stage—a preparation, from the mouth of a loving God to create a perfect home for those He would create in His image. Even the word pattern tends to shift when describing the sixth day. It does not say, "And God said let there be man. And it was so." Instead, we are given details on how God first formulated His plan for the creation of man and then how He executed that plan:

> Then God said, "Let Us make man in our image, according to our likeness; let them have dominion over the fish of the sea, over the birds of the air, and over the cattle, over all the earth and over every creeping thing that creeps on the earth." So God created man in his own image; in the image of God He created him; male and female He created them. Then God blessed them, and God said to them, *"Be fruitful and multiply; fill the earth and subdue it; have dominion over the fish of the sea, over the birds of the air, and over every living thing that moves on the earth."* (Genesis 1:26–28, italics added)

# Subdue the Earth

The command from the Father to have dominion and subdue the earth is often referred to as the "cultural mandate" and is connected with man being formed in the image of God. I like to call it the "first Great Commission." Day six is the climax of the creation week, and the two fundamental principles of that day are "dominion" and "image," but the presupposition to these two points is the command to "be fruitful and multiply." So enters the purpose of family in human history. Man is to be fruitful in order to multiply; he must multiply in order to fill the earth; and he must fill the earth in order to subdue it. Man is to be fruitful to reproduce a powerful force over all the earth.

The words dominion and subdue can often have a militaristic tone. They can certainly be intimidating and have often been a source of confusion. The term "dominion" means "benevolent leader." It also means to exchange or interchange information. A benevolent leader will prioritize learning about those whom he is leading, in order to become a more effective leader. There is an undeniable connection between the command to have dominion and man's nature as bearing the image of God. The connection is explicit: "Let Us make man in Our image … and let them have dominion." The actual Hebrew understanding of this is "Let Us make man in Our image … *in order* that they may have dominion" (italics added).

Subdue means "to put under your feet," or literally, "footstool." To be like God, to bear His likeness, means to have the authority to subdue the earth. To have dominion and to subdue the earth is not divisive or controlling; it is not arrogant or dismissive. It is the actual expression of heaven on earth, through God's people, in whom He chose to display His image. This truth needs to be embraced by every believer, and this banner needs to be above every home and family.

The family cultural mandate is the climax and focus of God's creative work, as described in Genesis 1. Everything about creation points and builds toward this first and fundamental command. All the previous days of creation— man's being made in God's image, the command to multiply, and even the cessation of God's work immediately afterward— point toward and highlight the importance and purpose of mankind to "subdue the earth." Families would be the means to that end.

# To Genesis and Beyond

The importance and significance of this first Great Commission is not limited only to the first chapter of Genesis. The instruction to subdue the earth is repeated frequently in the wider context of the book of Genesis, emphasizing its foundational importance. If Genesis 1 is the prologue, then Genesis can be broken down into ten other sections. The beginning of each of these ten sections is marked by the significant phrase, "these are the generations of." Genesis 2:4 begins, "These are the generations of the heavens and the earth once they had been created," and then the story of the garden of Eden and the fall of man begins. The other nine sections are introduced as the "generations" of Adam, Noah, the sons of Noah, Shem, Terah, Ishmael, Isaac, Esau, and Jacob. This forms the basic outline of the book of Genesis.

The significance of the mandate to subdue the earth is made plain in the context of what happens following the command. The immediate task was for Adam and Eve to attend and care for the garden of Eden. Their children were then to go into the earth and reproduce the culture of the garden across the world. The book of Genesis recounts how man responds to the command to fill the earth and to subdue it. The context of the whole book of Genesis, then, was a description and consequence of how man was unfaithful in the fulfillment of his task. Even though we separated ourselves from God through sin and were disobedient in following the mandate, it did not cancel the original and foundational message from God to his creation.

Genesis 9:1–2, 7 says, "So God blessed Noah and his sons, and said to them: *'Be fruitful and multiply, and fill the earth.* And the fear of you and the dread of you shall be on every beast of the earth, on every bird of the air, on all that move on the earth, and on all the fish of the sea. They are given into your hand ... And as for you, *be fruitful and multiply*; bring forth abundantly in the earth and multiply in it'" (italics added).

With a loving Father's heart, the Lord began to set apart a people to once again establish relationship. He would do this through covenant and, once again, through family. He would give a family His name, and He would be referred to as the God of Abraham, Isaac, and Jacob.

God discusses this covenant with Abraham, as mentioned in Genesis 17:2–6, where it says, "'I will make my covenant between Me and you and will multiply you exceedingly.' Then Abram fell on his face and God talked with him, saying: 'as for Me, behold, My covenant is with you and you shall be a Father of many nations. No longer shall your name be called Abram, but your name shall be Abraham for I have made you a Father of many nations. I will make you exceedingly *fruitful*; and I will make nations of you, and kings shall come from you'" (italics added).

In Genesis 35:10–12, it says, "God said to him, 'Your name is Jacob; your name shall not be called Jacob anymore, but Israel shall be your name.' So he called his name Israel. And God said to him: 'I am God Almighty. *Be fruitful and multiply*; a nation and a company of nations shall proceed from you, and kings shall come from your body. The land which I gave Abraham and Isaac I give to you and to your descendants after you I give this land'" (italics added).

This original mandate was never canceled. It would continue to be infused through the book of Genesis as a foundation for those created in His image. Even beyond the book of Genesis, as the story of God's people continues, in Leviticus 26:9, it says, "For I will look on you favorably and *make you fruitful, multiply you* and confirm My covenant with you" (italics added).

The mandate, once spoken, persists through time and even to this very day.

# The Pivotal Point

If you are not yet convinced as to the importance of this cultural mandate and the role of family, the most compelling evidence is yet to come. While it is clear that the mandate to subdue the earth is the climax of the creation week and even foundational for the history of mankind in the book of Genesis, there is even a greater context in which this cultural mandate should be seen. It is the context of God's special revelation to man, recorded throughout the Bible.

God's revelation to man is always progressive. It is progressive in the sense that it moves steadily forward, not progressive in the sense that it leaves behind what went before it. Every new addition of revelation that God leaves for man presupposes and builds on the knowledge that went before it. New revelation does not replace the promises and commandments that went before; rather, it builds upon them as a foundation. Each new message of God's revelation builds one upon the other.

When you look at the cultural mandate from this point of view, it is astonishing! The very first revelation of God to man is the cornerstone—the foundation of all subsequent revelation—and it was simply this: "Fill the earth and subdue it."

In his article "The Foundational Command: Subdue the Earth!" Dr. Albert M. Wolters, emeritus professor of religion at Redeemer University College in Ancaster, Ontario, writes:

> It [the cultural mandate] is the first and primary revelation, in the first and primary command. God is not a person to go back on a word once spoken, He is not one to countermand an order once given, for He is a constant God. And it is therefore of the greatest importance to keep that first, foundational word in mind when we listen to the many subsequent words which God addresses to man. All other revelation presupposes this. The history of God's progressive self-revelation can be

compared, in a very legitimate sense, to an inverted pyramid. Everything is poised, is pivoted upon, a single focal point upon which the whole structure rests. And that pivotal point is the cultural mandate.

It may be easy to lose sight of the original plan and heart of God because of what happened after Genesis 2. Sin, in a sense, dominates the storyline, and we become focused on the history of redemption from sin that culminates in Christ. However, redemption means restoration—a restoration back to original freedom. Christ's work is a restoration to our original task. The Father's original mandate was the first Great Commission. Christ's victory, lordship, and the proclamation of the second Great Commission (giving us His authority) was actually affirmation of the original mandate. We cannot operate in and fulfill the second Great Commission (Matthew 28: 19,20) until we have restored the first.

Dr. Wolters continues:

> We can say that the command to subdue the earth assumes importance of ever–widening dimensions, as we examine it in the successive concentric circles of its biblical context. If we take the context of the sixth day, this command appears to be the focus, if we take the context of the creation story, this command shows up as the climax, if we take the context of Genesis as a whole, this command is the cue for the drama of history; if we take the context of the whole history of God's special revelation, this command turns out to be the foundation of the

whole. It seems almost impossible to overemphasize the importance of this first and fundamental command of God to man.

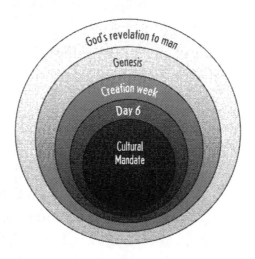

We can't overemphasize the importance of family in the implementing of God's plan. If the first step of restoration is to learn something's inherent value, then family has indescribable worth. It not only speaks to the importance of family units becoming restored and healed, but it also speaks to family as the means of restoration to the world. Families are to be strong, powerful, and healthy. They are to reflect the very image of God by whom they were created. When this occurs, family can reproduce, be sent, have dominion, and resume the task for which they were created. The earth will be subdued by the overwhelming love and presence of Father God, displayed through Christian families.

Our loving, infinite Father had an original plan for family, and the family was the original plan. In His wisdom, He created the world "unsubdued." He didn't create the world unsubdued so that we would fail. He did this for us, so we could be involved on an intimate level with a loving Father. He is perfect and powerful, and this first original mandate to God's families is available for you today.

The value of family is beyond measure, as convincingly demonstrated in chapter 1 of Genesis, but to know what family originally looked, like we must now explore chapter 2.

# There's No Place Like Home

I am so grateful for chapter 2 of Genesis. Chapter 2 takes an expanded look at day six of creation. It speaks to the importance of day six in the narrative. It tells the specifics of day six and the inherent value of the created man and woman. I think is also special that Scripture includes a description of what a loving Father created for His children prior to the effects of sin. The almighty God could have created anything for His children, and chapter 2 describes what He chose to create. A simple survey and dissection of this narrative provides us with a perfect picture of what family was originally supposed to look like and a demonstration of a loving Father creating a perfect home.

> This is the history of the heavens and the earth when they were created, in the day that the Lord God made the earth and the heavens, before any plant of the field was in the earth and before any herb of the field had grown. For the Lord God had not caused it to rain on the earth, and there

was no man to till the ground; but a mist went up from the earth and watered the whole face of the ground. And the Lord God formed man of the dust of the ground, and breathed into his nostrils the breath of life; and man became a living being. The Lord God planted a garden eastward in Eden, and there He put the man whom He had formed. And out of the ground the Lord God made every tree grow that is pleasant to the sight and good for food. The tree of life was also in the midst of the garden, and the tree of the knowledge of good and evil. Now a river went out of Eden to water the garden, and from there it parted and became four riverheads. The name of the first is Pishon; it is the one which skirts the whole land of Havilah, where there is gold. And the gold of that land is good. Bdellium and the onyx stone are there. The name of the second river is Gihon; it is the one which goes around the whole land of Cush. The name of the third river is Hiddekel; it is the one which goes toward the east of Assyria. The fourth river is the Euphrates. Then the Lord God took the man and put him in the garden of Eden to tend and keep it. And the Lord God commanded the man, saying, "Of every tree of the garden you may freely eat; but of the tree of the knowledge of good and evil you shall not eat, for in the day that you eat of it you shall surely die." And the Lord God said, "It is not good that man should be alone; I will make him a helper comparable to him." Out of the ground the Lord God formed every beast of the field and every bird of the air, and brought them to Adam to see what he would call them. And whatever Adam called each living creature, that was its name. So Adam gave names to all cattle, to the birds of the air, and to every beast of the field. But for Adam there was not found a helper comparable to him. And the Lord God caused a deep sleep to fall on Adam, and he slept; and He took one of his ribs, and closed up the flesh in its place. Then the rib which the Lord God had taken from man He made into a woman, and He brought her to the man. And Adam said: "This is now bone of my bones And flesh of my flesh; She shall be called Woman, Because she was taken out of Man." Therefore a man shall leave his father and mother and be joined to his wife, and they shall become one flesh. And they were both naked, the man and his wife, and were not ashamed. (Genesis 2:4–25)

This is a beautiful picture of a loving Father paying such close attention to the details of the needs of His children. He spared nothing, and His children not only had access to His garden but to His very presence. A culture was created that can be used by each family as a structure or template, as we all aspire to create a loving home.

# Take a Look Inside

The strategic aspects of the culture in the garden begins in Genesis 2:7, when it describes how the Lord God breathed the breath of life into the nostrils of man, and he became a living being. As mentioned previously, the man and woman were the pinnacle, the climax of creation week. The garden of Eden was a place of *life*. Our homes are to be a place where we can grow and thrive. Man wasn't just created, but he was given life. All of our words and actions in a loving home are to build up and to promote. The goal is always life and life more abundantly.

Genesis 2:8–14 describes a garden with *boundaries*. The garden of Eden was created just big enough for Adam and Eve. They were to tend and keep the garden, and their children were then to expand the garden and make the rest of the world look like the garden of Eden. The Father did not give Adam and Eve more than they could handle, and they were not to subdue what didn't belong to them. This is a wonderful demonstration of Christian homes operating with boundaries. It is loving parents who place boundaries around their children for their protection and security. The modern family has too often tried to create a boundary-less culture that unfortunately has led to woundedness and despair. Even the most eager and faithful ministers have suffered burnout and exhaustion because of living outside of boundaries. We need to return to the culture of the garden, where we ask our loving Father, "What is ours to tend and keep?"

The garden was a place of *provision*. Genesis 2:9 says that the land provided to Adam and Eve was filled with seed, food, precious metals, and gemstones. It was a place of extravagance. It was a place of more than enough. The loving Father not only created a home with work and task, but He also provided abundant provision to accomplish it. The Father gave man and woman a vision and a plan (the cultural mandate) and then provided for their vision. Fathers and mothers should always support the vision of their children. They should be "pro-vision." Children are never more secure than when parents provide for them and believe in them.

Genesis 2:16–17 demonstrates that the garden was a place of *rules, authority, and structure*. As mentioned previously, the Father operated in a clear authority structure. The heavenly Father had all dominion and created man in His image so that he could have dominion on the earth. The Father clearly placed His children in charge and afforded them tasks to do on the earth. He did, however, provide them with rules and structure on how (and how not) the garden should operate. Because He was true to His plan, He gave mankind free will to obey or not obey. He provided structure with the reward for obedience, and the consequences if they chose to disobey. He was, and is, and will always be a just and fair God.

These two verses also demonstrated that the garden was a place of *truth*. This is confirmed in Genesis 3:4, when they chose to disobey the rules of the Father. Satan tried to convince Adam and Eve that the Almighty God was not being truthful. They found out He is the Father of truth, and Satan is the father of lies. Christian homes should demonstrate that the fruit of our lips is always truthful and honorable. Christian parents need to be faithful in creating structure, authority, and rules and in the execution of the consequences for disobedience. Even before sin entered the earth, rules, authority, and structure were lovingly in place and should be foundational for every Christian home.

We also need to understand and be able to defend that all of Scripture is true. The dependability and authority of Scripture is being undermined in all society. Our children need to clearly understand and value their origin and their biblical worldview. Jesus is the Truth (John 18:37) and His words are truth.

An exciting portion of the first home created by our loving Father is found in Genesis 2:15, 19–20. Family was created with *purpose and task.* They were to tend and keep the garden, have dominion, and interchange with creation. Adam was to name the animals and release them into their destiny. They were to be loving, benevolent rulers. Perhaps more important, they were to be fruitful; to raise children in the culture of the garden, so that they, in turn, could be benevolent rulers over the whole earth.

If you are like I am, you don't get very excited about the picture of heaven where we lounge in white robes, plucking on a harp. This is because we were created with task and purpose. I am so excited that I am meant to be part of a family and am meant to raise my children to be a family with passion and purpose.

Covenant was established before creation with the heavenly family as the perfect trinity. As my mother, Heather

Claussen, explains in her book, *Stepping Stones: God's Covenant Plan through the Ages*, they operated in perfect "tri-unity," and "It was simply too good to keep to themselves!" It was from this Spirit that God said in Genesis 1:26, "Let *us* make man in our image, according to our likeness; let *them* have dominion …" (italics added). Covenant was in place from *before* the foundations of the earth and is available to us today.

Covenant was introduced to families in Genesis 2:18–24. The only thing the Father said that was "not good" during creation week was that man was alone. Man and woman were to be the complete demonstration of the Father on earth. So covenant was demonstrated between a man and a woman. To demonstrate the strength of the covenant relationship, they were not simply two pieces of a puzzle, fit nicely together, but rather "one flesh." This marriage relationship would demonstrate oneness and demonstrate the simple premise of covenant: "All that I have is yours and all that you have is mine." This covenant was then offered to the family in the presence of a loving God. After the fall, the same loving Father would use this very premise of covenant to continue relationship with His chosen people. Covenant is relational, unbreakable, and foundational to every family. Covenant began before the garden and is still central today in your relationship with your God, your spouse, and your family.

Genesis 2:25 demonstrates that the garden was a place of *transparency, freedom, and joy.* Adam and Eve were naked and were not ashamed. Fear and shame were counter-cultural in the garden. Intimacy and transparency were central to God's plan, and our homes should be a place where we don't have to hide. Home should be a place of laughter and joy. True freedom is not found outside of boundaries; true freedom is found when we can be all we were created to be, without reservation, within the confines of loving boundaries. Shame is defeated by a family culture that shows unconditional love and is restorative in nature. It is time for Christian families to be, once again, (metaphorically) naked. The demonstration of transparency, freedom, and joy can be the most powerful force of influence on the face of the earth.

Finally—and most important—demonstrated throughout chapter 2 and redemonstrated in Genesis 3:8, the garden was a place of *relationship and presence.* The whole point— the very premise, the entire purpose—of creation and the garden was a loving Father in relationship with His created children. Our God is a relational God. He is not far off and removed. He left us in charge, but He did not leave us alone. Everything discussed in Genesis 2 is wonderful and nice, but if it doesn't lead us into relationship and into appreciation of His presence, then it is *nothing.* It is all about His presence! The culture in the garden was the Lord God, walking in their very presence in the "cool of the day."

# End of Story

This was to be the end of the story. Scripture, in a sense, was meant to be two chapters long. There would need to be no further explanation, because our very source of life would be walking with us in the cool of the day. Everything we do—every prayer, every action, and even every word of Scripture—is to lead us into relationship.

Relationship and presence with the Father is the absolute key to a loving home. When separation occurred because of sin, we would expect to see all other conditions of the home, based on His presence, fall away. Too often, that is exactly what we see today.

He not only desires to have a relationship with us, but He clearly designed us to be in relationship with others. It is still not good for us to be alone. The nuclear family is so clearly an earthly demonstration of the heavenly family. Families are to be the bearers of God's image, of His light on the earth. This is what He intended from the foundations of the earth.

Restoring relationship with our heavenly Father is central to this entire book and our ministry. When our identity is secure as sons and daughters, this, in turn, creates alignment to all of our relationships in our families. What we have discovered is that family is incredibly important and essential. Restoration of family relationships is key to the restoration of the world. This has to be true, because this was God's original plan.

The restoration of family is so vitally important because of its immense inherent value. It is worth restoring because we have a picture of what it originally looked like … and it is beautiful! It is worth restoring, because the world needs Christian families to be all they were created to be. This is attainable. All was not lost in the garden.

We know that the Bible is longer than two chapters and that all of mankind was thrown into a tailspin because of

Genesis 3, but as soon as sin entered the world, our loving Father put His plan into place for restoration. He is so loving and relational that He didn't want to be separated from us. In the next chapter, I will explain why the Father sent Jesus on a restoration mission. Because of the resurrection power of Jesus, the culture of the garden and of the family is not dead.

# Chapter 2: Atomic Clock

## *When the Fullness of Time Had Come*

Just like with the Bible, this book can't end with the garden. God's plan for mankind and for family is so beautiful that we would love to just stay and study that culture forever. We know, however, that Genesis 3 happens. Despite the tragedy of sin, it does mark the beginning of the greatest love story ever told.

Before the story unfolds, let me explain in more detail the environment of the garden. This detail will help put in perspective the backdrop and consequences of the fall.

First, Adam and Eve were genetically perfect. The notion of a lesser-evolved, grunting caveman is preposterous. They were, perhaps, the most perfect, intelligent beings ever to walk the face of the earth. They not only were perfect physical specimens but had access to the Tree of Life, the fruit of which would allow their bodies to never break down and to live forever. This super-food probably had some unfathomable antioxidant properties that would prevent cellular breakdown. They also lived in the culture and environment where there was no disease, sickness, or other effects of sin.

I do believe, however, that Adam and Eve could be injured. I believe they had a highly acute nervous system and could feel and sense pain. Our bodies were created to sense pain, and it's a wonderful gift. There are disease processes known today, in which people do not sense pain, and their life expectancy is quite short. I believe, for example, that Adam could have worked in his field, stepped in a hole, and broken his ankle. This event was not the result of sin, and these events would not result in death. In this example, Adam's immune system would be so strong and effective that this fractured bone would most likely be healed in a matter of hours. Also, because of his close communion with the almighty Creator, the presence of the Lord would simply have resulted in Adam's rapid healing. This healing in the garden, at that time, would not have been considered supernatural, only natural.

Second, everything was provided through seed, according to Genesis 1:29. I believe even the Tree of Life provided seed that would then be taken by Adam and Eve's children and planted throughout the world, so that all would live forever in the expanded garden, and the earth would be subdued.

The importance of day 6 of creation was explained in detail in the previous chapter of this book, but I believe the seventh day is also very important. There is great significance in God creating the world, declaring that it was good, setting mankind in charge, and then resting. Everything was set into place according to His perfect plan during the week of creation.

Every living being and every seed was created that week, and from what I can tell, there has been no further creation apart from the original seed. Plenty of "creative" miracles took place throughout the Bible, but they all seem to have a seed or a substrate from which the miracle took place. For example, Jesus didn't just feed the five thousand; He multiplied the fish and the loaves. He didn't just create wine; He turned water into wine. When faced with a broken, crippled man, He didn't create a new man; He brought restoration to the man's body. This demonstrates the perfection of creation week and also demonstrates the constancy of God. We don't have the power, despite our sin and error, to cancel or derail what the Lord has set in place.

All was created, and then He was done. He is a God of His Word and a God of order. He was, and is, and will always be on His throne and in charge. There is no need for re-creation, only restoration. That is why understanding the culture, environment, and plan of the garden is so important as we pursue restoration.

Finally, prior to the fall, there was no knowledge of good and evil. For reasons I do not understand, Satan also was present in the garden. It seems that despite his rebellion toward God, he was afforded residence on the earth. He was, however, similar to all of the other created beings—subject to the rule and reign of mankind. Clearly, Satan operated in evil. His evil, however, was to have no effect. There was no knowledge of good and evil. He was present in the garden, but he was of no effect. The only way Satan could gain authority would be if mankind gave it to him—and that is exactly what happened. The culture of the garden was supposed to be mankind ruling with loving dominion and ruling in the presence of enemies.

# The Introduction of Enmity

With the environment of the garden as a backdrop, we now approach Genesis 3. I believe this understanding will help clarify the Father's reaction to the three offenders. Genesis 3 is often referred to as the "fall of man" or "the curse." Now that we understand the culture and condition of the garden in its purest form, unaffected by sin and corruption, it will help us contrast the new culture and conditions set forth in the curse.

When the Lord addressed the three offenders in what is referred to as the curse, I believe He did not say, "Because you have done this, I am very angry, and because I am so angry with you, I will place this curse upon you." Rather, I believe He brought a declaration as to the consequence of their actions. Now that sin had entered the world, the culture of the garden was changed. Contained in the curse was an explanation of what would take place, now that the loving Father was separated from His children. A chasm was formed between a holy God and an unholy people. No longer would they be able to enjoy the abiding presence of the Father, and Genesis 3 is the description of the Father's heartbreak.

> And they heard the sound of the Lord God walking in the garden in the cool of the day, and Adam and his wife hid themselves from the presence of the Lord God among the trees of the Garden. Then the

Lord God called to Adam and said to him, "Where are you?" So he said, "I heard your voice in the garden, and I was afraid because I was naked and I hid myself." And He said, "Who told you that you were naked? Have you eaten from the tree of which I commanded you that you should not eat?" The man said, "The woman whom you gave to be with me, she gave me of the tree and I ate." And the Lord God said to the woman, "What is this you have done?" The woman said, "The serpent deceived me and I ate." (Genesis 3:8)

When I used to read this passage of Scripture, I would interpret this with anger and disappointment in the Lord's voice. Now, with improved understanding of the Father's heart, I feel His anguish. There was heartbreak in the Daddy's voice when He asked, "Who told you that you were naked?"

Sin now had entered the world, and the culture of God's creation shifted. Everything was unable to stay the same. The Father readdressed His creation and explained the consequences of their actions: "So the Lord God said to the serpent: 'because you have done this, you are cursed more than all cattle, and more than every beast of the field; on your belly you shall go, and you shall eat dust all the days of your life. And I will put *enmity* between you and the woman, and between your seed and her Seed; He shall bruise your head, and you shall bruise His heel'" (Genesis 3:14,15, italics added).

Because of his deception, Satan could no longer live in anonymity. Satan was now marked for destruction, and the clock is ticking. Enmity was introduced into creation. All who would be born thereafter would be born into the kingdom of this world and into the culture of enmity. The authority that was intended for mankind has been passed to the serpent. But from the seed of the very woman he deceived, the Father put the restoration plan into motion. Because of his extravagant love toward His creation, He would use their seed to bring wholeness and restoration to the world. He is a God of restoration!

"To the woman He said: 'I will greatly multiply your sorrow and your conception; in pain you shall bring forth children; your desire shall be for your husband, and he shall rule over you'" (Genesis 3:16).

My interpretation of this passage will most likely be very different from the common interpretation. Traditionally, this has been interpreted as if prior to the fall pain in childbirth was not intended, but now, because of the curse and the anger of God, babies would be born with tremendous pain for the mother. I believe this is not the pain referred to in Genesis 3:16. As mentioned previously, Eve had a normal, functioning human body, with an intact nervous system. Labor pains, though excruciating, are a natural and an important part of the birthing process. The protective insulated process of pregnancy cannot be the same environment during delivery. Contractions are an important signaling mechanism of the shift that takes place physiologically within a woman's body. The dilation of tissues will trigger pain, and that pain will carry and direct the woman through the process to the joyful delivery. Although I'm a man and will never have to experience the labor process, I feel that this was not the result of the curse.

I believe the cultural change that took place in the garden after the fall was much more painful. It says in the passage that *there will be pain and sorrow in bringing forth children and in conception.* The fruit of the womb will be delivered into a world of enmity. The pain the woman will experience will be from the enmity of her offspring. What was initially intended to operate in unity will now operate in enmity. Her offspring, separated from the loving Father, will bring a mother's heart sorrow. Her children were intended to expand the garden and to operate with purpose, task, and loving dominion, but now, their culture will be of selfish gain and a murderous spirit. Eve would experience this pain within the first generation of her offspring, when Cain killed Abel. Family now meant pain and sorrow. A mother's heart could feel no greater pain than this.

Second, she also was warned regarding her desire for her husband. The culture of the garden would have the marriage relationship operating in complete unity, referred to as one flesh. Her relationship with her loving Father was her primary reference point, and there needed to be no other. Adam and Eve were to operate in complete unity, as they would fulfill their task on the earth. Now, because of the separation, she would have a tendency to make her relationship with her husband her primary reference point. Her value, significance, and security would hinge on the man's response to her, instead of the Father's love.

> Then to Adam He said, "Because you have heeded the voice of your wife, and have eaten from the tree of which I commanded you saying, 'you shall not eat of it': cursed is the ground for your sake; in toil you shall eat of it all the days of your life. Both thorns and thistles it shall bring forth for you, and you shall eat the herb of the field. In the sweat of your face you shall eat bread till you return to the ground, for out of it you were taken; for dust you are, and to dust you shall return." (Genesis 3:17-19)

As mentioned previously, I don't believe that thorns and thistles were created at the time of the fall. I believe they were created during creation week. Adam was in charge of the fields, He was to tend the fields, and they would willingly yield their fruit. However, I believe a shift took place when sin entered the world and enmity was introduced between man and creation. I believe thorns and thistles existed prior to this declaration, but now they lived in enmity. They weren't intended to be in the fields, but now man lost his dominion and authority, and thorns and thistles would now be adversarial. The relationship between the animal kingdom and mankind would also be adversarial. No longer would the world be in divine order.

Finally, death was introduced into the world. Now, instead of living forever, Adam would return to the dust from which he was formed. An innocent animal was killed to make coverings for their nakedness. Murder and bloodshed was witnessed in the first generation. Because of compassion, the Lord placed a cherubim at the east of the garden of

Eden, which would not allow Adam and Eve to return to the garden, eat of the Tree of Life, or live forever in their sin. Sin removed them from the culture of the garden and from the very presence of God.

# A Father Separated

The Father is all about relationship, and because of the rebellion of mankind, He became separated from the creation that He loves. The Old Testament God is often inaccurately accused of being malicious, bloodthirsty, wrathful, and vengeful. But let me challenge you with this one important question: what would your countenance be like if your children were separated from you? How would you respond if your children were abducted or manipulated and influenced away from your presence? What would you do to get them back? The love we have for our children is but a fraction of the pure almighty love of the heavenly Father. So begins the journey of this very Father to bring His children home!

The story moves on from the garden into the rest of the book of Genesis. God sets apart a people who would become His through covenant. Through the family of Abraham, Isaac, and Jacob, Israel would ultimately become a great nation, and from *this* nation would come *the* Seed, Jesus Christ. The remainder of the Old Testament is a loving story of a Father trying desperately to connect with His children. This would be in the form of covenants, tabernacles, arks, and veils. The Old Testament would be marred with repeated hard-heartedness and disappointments. His children would keep their distance and their stubborn, stiff-necked ways. But this never kept the Father from pursuing them.

In Galatians 4:3, it says, "Even so we, when we were children, were in bondage under the elements of the world. But *when the fullness of time had come*, God sent forth his son, born of a woman, born under the law, to redeem those who were under the law that we might receive the adoption as sons" (italics added).

It would seem as if the Father simply couldn't wait any longer. He couldn't live one more minute separated from His children. When the "fullness of time" had come, He sent His Son. He sent His Son on a restoration mission. Jesus became enmity for us, allowing Himself to be nailed to the cross and crucified, so that resurrection power could usher in the times of restoration of all things.

But what would He restore? He would restore the one thing that was the most important from the beginning of time: relationship and presence. The blood of Jesus would wash us and make us holy so that we could once again commune with our holy, loving Father. Remember, the rest of the culture of the garden would have no significance without His presence.

# Declaring a Father to an Orphan World

I'm concerned that the Christian Church today has become so salvation-focused that we have looked past the very central core of Jesus' mission. The Bible refers to Jesus as "the door" and as "the Way." My question is, "The door and the way to what?" To salvation? To everlasting life? To freedom from our sins? Of course! He provided all of these, and they should be celebrated our entire lives. The Bible is not referring to this, however. He is the door and the Way *back to the Father*!

The Lord told me that today's Christian Church is "dancing at the door." We've embraced the redemptive message of Christ but have missed the restorative message of Christ. We have become comfortable with the powerful and sacrificial life of Jesus, but the notion that we are to once again enter into a loving, intimate relationship with the Father has left many of us confused and intimidated.

> In the beginning was the Word, and the Word was with God, and the Word was God. He was in the beginning with God. All things were made through Him, and without Him nothing was made that was made. In Him was life, and the life was the light of men. And the light shines in the darkness, and the darkness did not comprehend it … He was in the world and the world was made through Him, and the world did not know Him. He came to his own and His own did not receive Him. But as many as received Him, to them He gave the *right to become children of God*, to those who believe in His name: who were born not of blood, nor of the will of the flesh, nor of the will of man, but of God. And the Word became flesh and dwelt among us, and we beheld His glory, the glory as of the only begotten of the Father, full of grace and truth … For the law was given through Moses, but grace and truth came through Jesus Christ. No one has seen God at any

time. The only begotten son, who is in the bosom of the Father, *He has declared Him.* (John 1:1–18, italics added)

The apostle John walked and ministered with Christ. He had one opportunity to introduce Christ in his book and could have written or emphasized anything. He could have talked about salvation or dying on the cross, but instead, he concluded, "He has declared Him." He declared who? He declared the Father! The remainder of the book of John is repeated declarations and reflections of Jesus to His Father.

I have highlighted in my Bible how often Jesus refers to His Father, and the vast majority of the book of John is highlighted. It has constant references to the Father. For example:

"Jesus said to them my food is to do the will of Him who sent me, and to finish His work" (John 4:34).

"Most assuredly I say to you the Son can do nothing of Himself for what He sees the Father do for whatever He does the Son also does in like manner" (John 5:19).

"I can of Myself do nothing. As I hear, I judge; and My judgment is righteous, because I do not seek my own will but the will of the Father who sent me" (John 5:30).

"You know neither Me nor my Father. If you had known Me you would have known my Father also" (John 8:19).

"I told you and you do not believe. The works that I do in my Father's name they bear witness of Me" (John 10:25).

"If I do not do the works of my Father do not believe Me; but if I do though you do not believe Me, believe the works that you may know and believe that the Father is in Me, and I in Him" (John 10:37).

"Do you not believe that I am in the Father, and the Father in Me? The words that I speak to you I do not speak on My own authority; but the Father who dwells in Me does the works" (John 14:10).

This is just a small sample from the book of John of Jesus' constant deflection to the Father. We can't miss the very thing He spent His life declaring. The life of Jesus was to declare a Father to an orphan world. If you have seen the merciful works of Jesus, then you have seen the very heart of the Father. Jesus didn't come to replace the Father. He came to restore our place in the Father.

# We Have a Target

My goal would never be to minimize the power of the blood of Jesus. Quite the contrary, my goal is to receive every inheritance that belongs to me because of the blood of my Savior. I rejoice every day that my sins are forgiven, my salvation is secure, and I get to enjoy everlasting life. However, the key to restoration, to restoring everything the Father originally intended for His children and families, is found in the loving embrace of our Father. Jesus made it possible to once again walk in the cool of the day in the presence of our Daddy. When the fullness of time came, God sent His Son not only to save us but to restore us.

We can once again return to the culture of the garden. On the cross, the Enemy was defeated. All authority in heaven and on earth was given to Jesus Christ. He, in turn, restored our dominion and rule on the earth. I believe that once again, families are the key to His plan. The earth is still unsubdued, and family is the central mechanism by which we will subdue the earth. However, it cannot be done apart from relationship.

It says in John 1:12, "But as many as received Him, to them He gave the right to become children of God to those who believe in His name …"

We have the right to once again become children in the home of a loving Father, which, of course, means we have the right to remain orphans.

Historically, Satan became the first orphan when he was separated from the very presence of the Father. He brought that orphan spirit into the world and used it to question the identity of Adam and Eve. Sin caused separation from the Father, and the world became orphaned.

It is this very orphan spirit that would fuel the enmity between relationships and all of mankind. It would weaken and distort the very fabric of what was intended to subdue the earth, that being family. Fatherlessness was the sinister plan of the Enemy from the very beginning and still is today.

However, we now have a target. *If* we embrace the importance of family, *if* we embrace the beautiful picture of what family was created to be, *if* we understand the tactics of the Enemy and his desire to undermine what God created in families, *if* we can fully embrace the truth that Jesus became enmity for us and paid the full price for our sin, so that we no longer have to approach our Father through a veil, and *if* we can stand up and declare that the family is worth it, *then* we have a target.

In the next chapter we will target the orphan spirit and how it influences and distorts every family relationship, which, as a result, has brought dysfunction to the church and all of society.

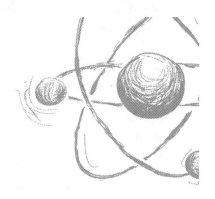

# Chapter 3: Core Meltdown
## *The Orphan Spirit*

We rejoice in a life that is saved, but the Father intended for us to have a life that is also victorious and restored. We are still His image-bearers on this earth. If we are to be His image-bearers, then our lives should be joyful, hopeful, and powerful.

After the resurrection, Jesus addressed His followers and released the second Great Commission. They were to "Teach all nations and baptize them in the name of the Father, the Son, and the Holy Spirit." This was the first time in Scripture that inferred that we were to have relationships with all three aspects of the Trinity. The relationship with the Son is that of grace and purpose, as we are given authority in His name. It is a baptism of grace. The relationship with the Holy Spirit is the baptism of power. It gives us the tools and weaponry to do the work. The foundational relationship is with the Father, and it is a baptism of love. It is from this baptism that we find our identity.

Paul summarizes this in his benediction at the end of 2 Corinthians, saying, "The grace of the Lord Jesus Christ, and the love of God, and the communion of the Holy Spirit be with you all. Amen" (2 Corinthians 13:14).

The world feels out of balance, because we, even as Christians, have things out of order. We first must pursue our positions, our identity. Once our identity is secured, then the Father will activate us as sons and daughters in our purpose. He will then provide us power to accomplish the purpose. First position, then purpose, and then power. We are intrigued and enamored at the proposition that we can live a Christian life with purpose and power. If we don't know who we are, however, we are orphaned.

When we received Jesus as our Savior, we became Christians. It is our allegiance, but it is not our identity. When we move and operate in the Holy Spirit, we are powerful and effective, but it is not our identity. Our identity is secured in the loving arms of our Daddy God.

# Identity Crisis

The orphaned Christian has an identity crisis. Every Christian receives Christ as an orphan, and they often "dance at the door," celebrating everything that Christ is to them, but they never enter. There is a loving Father waiting at the other side of the door, on His throne, and in His kingdom. In His kingdom there are restored relationships that allow us to once again subdue the earth. Yet often, because of fear and ignorance, we choose to stay orphans.

For multiple reasons, we view the Father as distant, unloving, vindictive and of questionable goodness. Because of this, we see Jesus as the safer alternative and continue to live our lives just waving the Christian flag, trying to do good, and performing for approval. Meanwhile, the earth is not being subdued, we are not taking dominion, and Christian marriages and families often don't look much different from those in the kingdom of the world.

The root issue is identity. The disease is the orphan spirit. Later in this book, I will discuss how we can once again restore the power to subdue the earth, but first, we must tackle the orphan spirit. This is the first step. What we have done up until this point has not been working. It is time to hit the reset button and realign ourselves with the Father's love.

If you are having or have had problems with any relationship, I would submit to you that at its root is a problem with your identity and the orphan spirit. When in the garden with the ever-abiding love of the Father, Adam and Eve's identity was secure, and their relationship was in perfect unity. If your culture has allowed disunity, mistrust, shame, and fear, then something still is orphaned. It is time to expose the orphan roots.

The best we can do as orphaned Christians is to fight over the issues of the day and proclaim all the things that we don't believe in. At the same time we are often unwilling to enter and influence society, because we are afraid and completely unaware that we have full access to a greater kingdom. The Father's kingdom has restored the kingdom of this world. We access His kingdom only as sons and daughters. We are not to just follow the Son but be a son.

When trying to bring healing and restoration to friendship, marriage, parenting, or family, we often may be guilty of chasing symptoms rather than discovering the root cause of the disease. We tend to trim the branches and ignore the root. For example, if someone comes into my office having gallbladder attacks, he would present with symptoms of bloating, nausea, abdominal pain, back pain, indigestion, and possibly diarrhea. I could very easily prescribe up to ten different medications that would help alleviate the symptoms, but none of these medications would help the root problem. The medications may help the patient feel better for a time, but unless my patient has his gallbladder removed, his problem will never be solved and will certainly become more serious with time.

So it is with the orphan spirit. For instance, someone can come to us with serious marital problems. Our temptation would be to look at the symptoms. There may be symptoms of anger, mistrust, poor communication, a critical spirit, and hopelessness. We may prescribe anger management or give homework to improve communication skills. These will no doubt help temporarily, but the root issue remains.

Similarly, in our society we look at all the problems that affect us today—problems such as violence, promiscuity, drug abuse, disrespect and dishonor, pornography, and even abortion plague our society. As Christians, we stand up against these symptoms; we march and protest. Again, we are missing the root issue. The disease is identity, and it affects every aspect of society. By attacking the symptoms, the Christian Church has unwittingly emboldened the social causes. Those who practice these things have coalesced and gathered around one another, and the social issues now have become their identity, and the problem grows.

We are all horrified at the rise of gun violence in our nation, especially in our schools. All we seem to do is focus our attention on the gun, as if further gun control will solve the problem. The problem is not the gun; the problem is the person holding the gun. This person has no hope, no value for his life or the lives of others, and he is lost without identity. Give him identity in the Father, and the gun problem will be solved.

Satan's tactics have never changed. Whether we are constantly critical toward our spouse, or we are holding a gun, about to enter a school, the Enemy inflicts us with doubt about our relationship with our Father. This is what he did in the garden of Eden when he had Adam and Eve question the intentions of their Father. He had them question their own identity as sons and daughters, and that is still his tactic today.

The orphan spirit is fueled by fatherlessness. As children, we enter this world relating to our natural fathers and mothers. There is no way to disconnect our attitudes and feelings toward our spiritual Father from our attitudes and feelings toward our natural fathers and mothers. Parenting has such a critical role in the shaping of a child's worldview and ultimately his or her outlook on the Father's love.

As I testified previously, I was raised in a very loving home. I never went to bed at night wondering if my parents loved me. My father demonstrated the Father's love very well, yet despite this, I still suffer with orphan issues, and I will be so bold as to say that most of you have root orphan issues as well. I will give you a strategy to not only overcome and displace these orphan issues but a strategy to steward your identity as a son or daughter.

# Orphan Spirit Defined

First, we must define the orphan spirit. The spirit entered the Garden and was introduced by the first orphan, Satan himself. The spirit had no authority or power on its own. It could only be activated and set in place by the one who had authority and dominion on the earth, and that was mankind. Adam and Eve were made in the image of God and were given dominion. The Father Himself breathed life into Adam's nostrils. When his eyes opened, the first thing he saw was his Papa. When Eve was formed and her eyes were opened, the first thing she saw was her Papa. They were in the very presence of God in the loving home that He created for them. Tragically, their sin caused separation, they became fatherless, and the world became orphaned.

Jack Frost, author of the book *Spiritual Slavery to Spiritual Sonship*, defines the orphan spirit as follows:

> The orphan spirit is a sneaking suspicion that you are rejected. If I am rejected, then I must be rejectable. An orphan heart or orphan spirit is characterized by a feeling of not belonging. It carries with it a deep-seated sense of not being accepted, valued, honored, or loved. It causes one to live life as if he does not have a safe and secure place in the Father's heart. He feels he has no place of affirmation, protection,

comfort, belonging, or affection. Self oriented, lonely, and inwardly isolated, he has no one from whom to draw godly inheritance.

Often within the church, it is difficult to tell whether a person walks in the heart attitude of an orphan or a son. Outwardly, a person may have a pattern of service, sacrifice, discipline, and apparent loyalty, but we do not know what is inside a person until he or she gets "bumped." Then the attitude of the heart overflows at a time when that person feels he is not receiving the recognition or favor he deserves. Somehow, the difference lies in the motives and intentions of the heart.

Jack Frost also developed a worksheet that defines and demonstrates a heart of an orphan contrasted with the heart of Sonship. (This is available at familyrestorationproject.com.) I will share a few highlights:

The orphan sees God as a master, whereas the son sees God as a loving Father.

The orphan is independent and self-reliant, whereas the son is interdependent and acknowledges his need.

The orphan strives for the praise, approval, and acceptance of man, whereas the son is totally accepted in God's love and justified by grace.

The orphan suffers from self rejection from comparing himself to others, whereas the son has a positive self image and is affirmed because he knows he has such value to God.

The orphan seeks comfort in counterfeit affections such as addictions, compulsions, escapism, busyness, or hyper religious activity, whereas the son seeks to rest in the Father's presence and love.

The orphan faces his peers with competition and rivalry, while harboring jealousy toward others' success and position; whereas the son operates in humility and unity as he values others and is able to rejoice in their blessings and successes.

Orphans see authority as a source of pain; distrustful toward them and lack a spirit of submission, whereas the son respects authority, is honoring, and sees authority as ministers of God for good in his life.

The orphan is guarded and conditional towards love, and receives love based upon others' performance as he seeks to get his own needs met, whereas the son is open, patient, and affectionate as he lays his life and agendas down in order to serve others.

The orphan operates in bondage where the son operates in liberty.

This is not the entire list, and still it is almost impossible to not see ourselves in one of the orphan characteristics. In summary, the orphan spirit is based on others' ability to meet our needs.

# The Downward Spiral

The life of a spiritual orphan is fueled by disconnection with a father. It creates a downward spiral: I have no father, so I have no identity. I have no identity, so I have no purpose. I have no purpose, so I have no direction. I have no direction, so I have no destiny. I have no destiny, so I have no hope. The ultimate result of living as a spiritual orphan is hopelessness.

We can look at the lives of Elvis Presley, Michael Jackson, and Whitney Houston. These three singers had very much in common. Very few would argue that they obtained the very highest level in their profession and status in the eyes of the world. So much so that all three are considered royalty. For instance, Elvis has been referred to as the "king of rock 'n' roll," and Jackson as the "king of pop." All three were raised with Christian influence, and all three would testify, at one point in their lives, to a saving knowledge of Christ. However, just like the Prodigal Son, they sought their identities outside of the Father's home. Each would strive and work to achieve everything that this world could offer, and their lives would represent the rare few who actually did achieve and obtain everything this world could provide—success, fame, money, attention, admiration, and unrivaled talent. Still to this day, Whitney Houston's voice can reduce me to tears.

All three had undeniable gifts that would attract millions. It can also be said that all three unfortunately shared a deep hopelessness. How hopeless it must feel to achieve everything that life can offer, only to find that it still cannot offer identity. It still can never satisfy. Their quest to find love and security outside of the Father's embrace was fruitless. All three eventually sought an anesthetic (drugs) to dull and numb the pain that was in their hearts, and it led to their destruction.

Their lives should serve as a warning to all of us who seek even a portion of what they were trying to obtain. It is just as dangerous to seek our identity in our professions, our money, our relationships, or even in our religion.

It seems counterintuitive for Christians to live in hopelessness. But that is what we see all over the world. Let's be clear: our salvation is secure. Jesus, on our behalf, has obtained victory. Unfortunately, often our lives are not victorious.

As sons and daughters, we listen to the Father's voice. Orphans, on the other hand, hear many different voices and are easily influenced by them. Unlike the Father's voice, these voices don't always have our best interests in mind. Because orphans hear many different voices, they often pick up what doesn't belong to them. In their desperation and need for identity and security, orphans will look to others to meet their needs that were meant to be satisfied by the Father. This, unfortunately, sets into motion relationships where people are trying to meet the needs of others that were never theirs to fill. I believe this is at the very core of the problems with families today. Marriages and families are dying all around us ... even Christian marriages and families.

# The Orphan Effect

Let me walk you through the natural progression of an orphaned Christian, either uncomfortable or unfamiliar with the Father's love. Throughout this book, I will introduce Jack and Jill. This could be the same Jack and Jill of nursery rhyme fame, because their life experience reflects many marriages and families today; when Jack fell down and broke his crown (sonship, identity, inheritance), Jill came tumbling after.

In the center, we have the orphan. In our example, Jack was a Christian. He had given his life to Jesus, and he understood the concept of grace and received that for himself. He attended church regularly, and the teaching he received at church was focused on the sacrificial life of Christ and the price that was paid for his sin. He was a sinner saved by grace, but he was never taught that this grace gave him the right to become a son (John 1:12). He was comfortable with the servant-and-soldier mentality in service to his King Jesus. He never was comfortable with the notion that he was a beloved son. His natural father was never comfortable with affection. Even though Jack knew his father loved him, his father never told him. Jack received acclamations and admiration from his parents when he performed well and always felt that their love was connected to his performance. His mistakes were always met with disapproving looks, shame, and at times, punishment. He struggled with identity and found his worth in his accomplishments. He had a hole at the core of his heart that only the Father could fill.

He desired to be loved and found some satisfaction when he won the heart of a beautiful young lady named Jill.

The next circle of life was created, and marriage covered his orphan state. For a time, this relationship met his needs. He felt loved, admired, and wanted. His wife's love was a soothing balm to his painful heart. Over time, however, her ability to meet his needs became more difficult. She was never created or intended to be his answer for the emptiness in his heart. He became more frustrated and disenchanted with her inability or unwillingness to meet these needs. His ability to find his identity as a husband slowly slipped away. They began to do things apart from one another and once again searched for fulfillment and joy in other areas of life. Their marriage, like many marriages, began to unravel.

Perhaps they could find a new sense of unity, purpose, and fulfillment in having children.

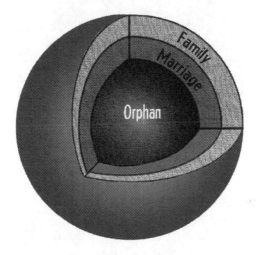

The next circle was formed as they became a family. Raising children ushered in a new season of fulfillment as they worked together. Perhaps the children would provide the love in his heart that he always needed. Very quickly, the joy and wonderment of having children was replaced by the stress and the responsibility of raising a family. Although he vowed to never be cold and removed, as his father was toward him, Jack, too, found himself uncomfortable with expressing love. This was never modeled for him. He too expressed anger and disappointment when his children performed less than he dreamed they would. His children became removed and at times rebellious, and they turned to their peers for their fulfillment, rather than their parents.

As a Christian, Jack knew where he could go for help. He turned to his local church to help with the brokenness of his family.

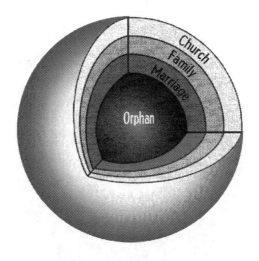

Church now had to become an even larger circle to try to cover this broken family. Jack made frequent calls to his pastor for prayer and advice. He complained about his wife and his children and their apparent lack of respect toward him. He was appreciative of any way the pastor could help them but became embittered and disgruntled when the pastor was unavailable.

The pastor of their church had big visions and dreams for their community, but because he was inundated with many families in strife and brokenness, all his energy was focused on his flock. He quickly became burned out and left the ministry. Although Jack knows Jesus as his

Savior, he could not understand why all those around him abandoned him and could not meet his needs. He deserved better than that.

Now that the local church was unable to meet the needs of the community, the local and federal government moved in and carried the needs of the poor, the widow, and the orphan. The pastor had a vision to meet these needs but was unable to fulfill it, due to the needs of his own congregation.

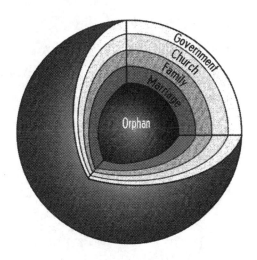

The government now has to be an all-encompassing circle, filling the needs of society that were never its to carry. Christians often accuse the government of overreaching while at the same time setting down what was given them to fulfill.

The government is in debt, yet it swallows up more of the responsibility of society. *The government has picked up what does not belong to it.* This is because the Christian Church has not fulfilled its obligation to care for those in their region. The church has been unable to fulfill this obligation because it has been too busy dealing with broken families and internal issues. It focuses too much of its time, energy, and resources on forming programs that will alleviate some of the symptoms of brokenness in families. *The church has picked up what does not belong to it.*

Children feel the weight and pressure of temptation outside the home and unmet expectations within the home. They are asked to meet the orphan expectations of their parents. *Children have been forced to pick up what does not belong to them.* Spouses hope that they will complete one another. They hope that the love they feel on their wedding day will sustain them "until death do us part." They become quickly disenchanted by their spouses' inability to meet their needs. *Husbands and wives have tried to pick up what does not belong to them.*

This brings us back to our orphan. Jack was despondent and frustrated. His only recourse was to find some hope and fulfillment elsewhere. He could find some escape in his career or in busyness. Too often, his escape was found in fantasy, the golf course, or in flirtation with other women.

This story is found within the Christian community. We cannot continue to focus on the symptoms alone. Too much time on the golf course or becoming a workaholic is not the problem; it is a symptom. I am tired of disappointment, dysfunction, and divorce. Something has to change! That something is found in the very message of Jesus Christ. It is found in what He came to declare. The cure for this disease is found in the loving embrace of a Father. Only a Father can heal an orphan heart.

The answer for your family is found in the answer of this one simple question: "Who are you?"

The answer is in identity. The orphan spirit is pervasive. It has been present on this earth since the garden of Eden. This spirit cannot be cast out. It must be displaced. Your answer and the hope for your family is found in the unconditional love of your Father. In this next chapter, I will introduce you to the heart of your Father, and you will be invited into His embrace!

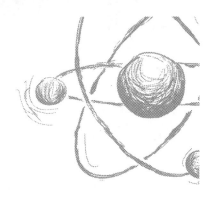

# Chapter 4: From Adam to Atom
## *Restoring the Power of Identity*

This message on displacing the orphan spirit comes directly from the transformational experiences that our family has had with the Father's love. We have had the same struggles with identity that your family has had, and we pray that you will experience the breakthrough that we have experienced.

For example, my wife, Amy, has a radical testimony of how her orphan heart was transformed by the extravagant love of her heavenly Father. Like most orphans, Amy felt that she needed to earn her Father's love. Her life was marked by achievement and the drive to "try harder" to achieve her Father's approval. On her own strength, this would be impossible to achieve, and she felt like she never measured up. Amy did not see Jesus as her pathway to the loving Father; she saw Jesus as the one who would protect her from an angry, disapproving Father. This cycle of performance and disappointment left her exhausted, despondent, and desperate. While Amy was attending a conference by Leif Hetland, he introduced to her the term "orphan spirit." The Holy Spirit whispered in Amy's ear, "That's you." She now had a target. The source of her emptiness and desperation had a name.

She would spend the next three days "on the carpet," repeating over and over again, "I love you, Daddy, and You love me!" She allowed the everlasting love of her Father to wash over her and displace the orphan spirit that was within her. This one moment brought radical transformation to Amy's life, to our marriage, and to our home.

Amy was raised in a loving home, but the orphan spirit is crafty. The Enemy will always use the tactic of challenging our identity to keep us separated from the Father's love.

I hope you are convinced of the pervasiveness of the orphan spirit. Furthermore, perhaps you recognize some of the symptoms in your own life. Perhaps you related to our orphan in the previous chapter. Perhaps you can relate to Amy's testimony. That is the first step toward your healing. Like anything we face in life, we must first acknowledge our own orphan issues, because then we have a target.

Displacing the orphan spirit is accomplished through the baptism of love. It is an experiential encounter with the loving embrace of the Father. It is the transition from displacing into embracing. Similar to experiencing Jesus or the Holy Spirit, often some basic teaching is required. But this process of receiving the Father's love requires minimal teaching and maximum receiving.

# The Countenance of the Father

First, as mentioned above, we need to acknowledge our own orphan issues. I hope that after reading the last chapter, some of the symptoms of an orphan connected with you. As with most things, it is always easier to see orphan issues in others. I would ask you to resist the temptation to do so. I encourage you to ask the Holy Spirit to illuminate in your life the things that are out of order. Ask Him to illuminate the relationships where you have required something from someone that was not theirs to give. I trust that the Holy Spirit will be faithful to illuminate these things in your life, until they are completely displaced.

Second, we must acknowledge that our past shapes our perspective. This is a painful prospect. It is practically impossible for someone who has been exposed to hurt, abuse, neglect, and shame to have this not impact his or her view of the heavenly Father. Even with my parents' extravagant love toward me, they were not perfect. No parents can ever be the perfect expression or representation of the heavenly Father's love. The breadth of human experience, in regards to family, spans from somewhere near my experience to the deepest, darkest places of hurt and cruelty. When confronted with the word "father," there will be a range of responses, from "love him" to "never knew him" to "hate him." There is little doubt that all of these experiences—the good, the bad, the triumph, and the tragedy—influence our understanding and paradigm of the Father.

We need to understand that the despair in family relationships was not meant to be that way. Mothers and fathers, prior to the fall, were supposed to be everything the children initially needed and be a pure expression of the Father's love. The sin and depravity of man has skewed this picture. I feel that we are entering a season where these relationships will be healed, but we must first deal with our own identity issues. We need to be able to look past the humanness of this world and our experiences, and discover the true heart of our heavenly Father.

I'm confident that through this process, you will be ushered into His very presence and feel His unconditional love for you. Before a wounded heart can be vulnerable before a loving God, it needs to understand that the Father is safe and loving.

You probably are familiar with the passage in Numbers 6:24–26 that says, "The Lord bless you and keep you; the Lord make His face shine upon you and be gracious to you; the Lord lift up His countenance upon you and give you peace."

How comfortable are you with the Lord's face? How comfortable are you with the Lord's countenance? Our experience may not always be that of a father with a loving countenance and a comforting face, a face that is pleased with us. Our experiences with our fathers may bring anything but peace. Perhaps you see your heavenly Father as one who is just waiting for you to make a mistake so that He can impart His wrath upon you.

This view of the Father is from the spirit of bondage. We are no longer under the spirit of bondage. We have been set free.

"For you did not receive the spirit of bondage again to fear, but you received the Spirit of adoption by whom we cry out, *"Abba, Father."* The Spirit himself bears witness with our spirit that we are children of God, and if children then heirs—heirs of God and joint heirs with Christ, if indeed we suffer with Him, that we may also be glorified together" (Romans 8:15–17, italics added).

The spirit of bondage is an Old Testament mind-set. The life, death, and resurrection of Jesus freed us from the spirit of bondage so that we now may enter into the spirit of adoption. It is from that spirit that we cry out, "Abba Father!"

"Abba" is the familiar, more casual word for father. It is the word a young Hebrew child would use for his father. It would be our equivalent of calling our father "daddy" or "papa." It is the word the Lord wants us to use when we call His name. When I come through the door after work, it would be silly for my children to greet me with, "Greetings, Father, how art thou?" No, instead, I come through the door to the screaming sound of "Daddy!" I wouldn't want it any other way, and the same is true of your heavenly Father.

The blood of Jesus was a game-changer. His wrath was satisfied, and the New Testament Father is in a good mood. Because of His Son, He has His children back ... and this changes everything!

In Luke 15 is the story of the prodigal son. Clearly, both of the sons in this story had orphan issues, but I do want to be clear. This story is not about the sons; it is about the Father. We are tempted to read Scripture from the spirit of bondage. We need to understand that the purpose of Scripture is not just to tell us what to do; it is to tell us who He is. The intention of all of Scripture is to bring us into relationship. If we read the story of the prodigal son from a spirit of bondage, then we view this story from a place of performance. The best we can pull out of the story is that no matter what we have done in our past, God is faithful to forgive and will accept us back. Although that is true, it is not the heart of the story. It is a story of a father separated from his son, a son who thought he could find his identity separate from his father's house. It is a story of a father who, when he saw his son far off, didn't stand there with his arms crossed, waiting for an apology; rather, he ran to him and threw his arms around him, because his son, who was separated, was now back home. The son would have been content to be a slave in his father's house, but the father would have nothing to do with that. Instead, the father restored his sonship and threw him a party.

You need to understand that the heavenly Father is in a partying mood. Because of His Son, Jesus, His children are back again. There is nothing we can do to earn the love of our Father … *He just wants us.* That is the countenance of your Father toward you.

The next step in allowing Him to displace the orphan spirit is the understanding that the Father smiles over you and is delighted in you. He is safe and loving. He is not afraid of your past, and just like the Prodigal Son, He is not afraid of the mess you have created. He just wants you.

I have had the privilege of delivering hundreds of babies and am always fascinated with the family dynamics that take place in the delivery room. Almost without exception, the father, although attentive to mother, tends to focus on me. The delivery process is often an anxious, loud, and sometimes bloody process. This can be quite intimidating, especially for a first-time father. He looks at my countenance. I always make it a point to have a smile on my face and a calm posture. I understand that all of the screaming, blood, fluids, and beeping monitors are normal. I am able to see the end from the beginning. So it is with the heavenly Father. Our lives may be chaotic and bloody, but He is not intimidated. He sees you as a son, and He knows the end from the beginning. He delights in what you are birthing and delights in the destiny of your life. His countenance is that of joy and peace over you.

# The Spirit of His Son

Even so we, when we were children, were in bondage under the elements of the world. But when the fullness of time had come, God sent forth His son, born of a woman, born under the law, to redeem those who were under the law, that we might receive the adoption as sons. And because you are sons, God has sent forth the *Spirit of His Son* into your hearts, crying out, "Abba, Father!" Therefore you are no longer a slave but a son and if a son, then an heir of God through Christ. (Galatians 4:3–7, italics added)

I believe the "Spirit of His Son" is the declaration of the Father. His message was to declare the Father (John 1:18). Jesus' mission was to bring us back into right relationship with the Father. When we receive that Spirit, when we believe that everything that Jesus did was from the very heart of the Father, then we cannot help but cry out, "Abba Father!" It is the very Spirit of Jesus within us that cries out from our spirit, "Daddy!"

If you are looking for an outward manifestation or a tangible sign that you have received the baptism of love, it will be found in your willingness, comfort, and ability to call him "Daddy." If there is something inside of you that feels innately uncomfortable with referring to your Father as Papa, I would submit to you, that you are still under the spirit of bondage. If you scoff at the notion or feel it is irreverent to refer to the almighty God as "Daddy," then you are still approaching him as a soldier or a slave, not as a son.

More excitement is found in Scripture as we continue to read from the "Spirit of His Son," rather than the spirit of bondage.

"The kingdom of heaven is like treasure hidden in the field which a man found and hid; and for joy over it he goes and sells all that he has and buys that field. Again, the kingdom of heaven is like a merchant seeking beautiful pearls, who, when he had found one pearl of great price, went and sold all that he had and bought it" (Matthew 13:44–45).

I have always read the Scripture from a spirit of bondage. I interpreted it as, "I must sell and sacrifice everything that I have for God's kingdom. His kingdom is so beautiful and valuable that I must sacrifice everything so that I can purchase what He has for me." This is preached in churches all over the world and is a servant mentality. I believe it is a misinterpretation of the Scripture. It doesn't say "we" are supposed to be like; it says the "kingdom of heaven is like."

Once again, Scripture isn't just to tell us what to do but to tell us who He is. Jesus came to declare the Father, and parables are to tell us what He is like. This may blow your mind and rattle your theology, but you need to understand that *you* are the treasure hidden in the field and *you* are the pearl of great price. The Father emptied heaven to come to rescue you. Jesus surrendered all that He had to purchase you. This is the heart of our loving God toward you!

He is crazy about you, because you are His son or daughter, and you are back home. The Father is in a partying mood. He delights and laughs over you! He sings and dances over you! There is nothing you can do that would remove you as a son or daughter.

# Who Am I?

This leads us back to the question at the end of the last chapter. I believe this is one of the most critical, impactful questions you can ask in your lifetime. The question is, "Who am I?"

If you randomly ask this question to people walking down the street, you most likely will get answers ranging from their given name to their occupation or allegiances. Some may even identify themselves with a political party, a social cause, or their sexual orientation.

So, "Who are you?" *You are a son (or daughter) of the Most High God!* That is who you are; that is your identity. It is from that identity that all of our relationships come back into alignment. It is from that identity that we find our security and peace. It is from that identity that we can lay down our striving and performing. It is from that identity that the hole in our hearts is filled by the only One who can fill it. It is from that identity that we find wholeness and healing. It is because of that identity that the loving Father never stopped pursuing us from the beginning of time.

*We must never move past the issue of identity.* We will be tempted to skip this, because it forces us to deal with some hurtful experiences. We will try to move on to the more exhilarating experiences of purpose and power, while abandoning our position. We may not understand that an orphan with power can hurt people. First position, then purpose, and then power. If it takes a lifetime to discover and rediscover our position in the Father, then it is worth the journey. Don't move past identity. Stay here until it becomes cellular—your DNA. The first Adam was able to experience "God with us"; the second Adam (Jesus) allowed us to experience "God in us." This identity needs to become our very being, our very atomic makeup, until it satisfies that hole in our hearts.

With our identities secured, we can come before our loving Father and ask Him to displace anything that is orphan within us. We can ask Him to baptize us in His love. If you are willing, you can start by repeating the following declarations:

- "Daddy, today is the day that everything changes."
- "Forgive me for partnering with the lies that say that I am a failure, that I can never measure up, that I will never succeed, and that I am unlovable."

- "I repent for agreeing with these lies. By the authority I have in Jesus, I command these lies and anything attached to them to get out of my life immediately and permanently, in Jesus' name."
- "Daddy, reveal to me anything that is holding me back from experiencing Your perfect love."
- "Daddy, reveal to me anyone whom I need to forgive."
- "Papa, I receive Your gift of love with gratitude and thanksgiving. Come and fill me with Your love right now. I want to feel You, know You, and touch You."
- "Now, Daddy, seal the gift You have given me today, that I may know I am eternally and outrageously loved forever."

Don't move past identity and His love. You may need to daily repeat these declarations until they truly come from your spirit. You need to allow the Father's love to wash over you and allow Him to encounter you. It will change everything!

# Steward Your Identity

Finally, we must steward our identity. The first Adam did not protect his identity as a created son of the Most High God. The second Adam was faced with the same temptation as the first. Satan questioned His identity. He repeatedly provoked Jesus with, "*If* you are the Son of God ..." Jesus, however, was ready. He knew who He was, and He knew from whom He received His power. What Satan was able to accomplish in the garden, he was not able to accomplish in the wilderness.

Satan is crafty, and he will try to cast doubt on your newfound identity. He will try to return you to the cycle of performance and entitlement. He will once again try to convince you that you are unworthy of the Father's love. You will need to steward this identity well, recognize your orphan tendencies, and not allow them a foothold.

For example, I recently delivered a message on the "Original Plan for Family and the Culture of the Garden of Eden" to a local ministry. Shortly thereafter, I attended a different local ministry but with a similar audience. Someone stood up and delivered a message that she had read; she thought it was profound and insightful. It was about the culture of the garden of Eden! Immediately, something rose up within me that wanted to be recognized, and I wanted those in the room to acknowledge that this was *my* message. Rather than be encouraged that my message was being confirmed, I felt prideful, possessive, and competitive. My identity was out of line, and my spirit was orphan. I am happy to report that I was able to detect the spirit rising within me. I quickly identified it, repented for not stewarding my identity, and was able to displace the spirit with the Father's love and be encouraged by the message.

The exciting part is that sonship offers more than just a healed heart. As mentioned in Romans and Galatians, we become joint heirs with Christ. As sons and daughters, we obtain an inheritance. Simply put, we inherit all of heaven. We not only get to approach the world and society with authority as sons and daughters, but we are allowed special access to the very heart of the Father.

In addition to this, when you have a secured identity as a son or daughter, this puts all your family relationships back into alignment. When families are restored back to what they were created to be, then—and only then—can they go back to the original task of subduing the earth. The next chapter will give an exciting picture of what families could look like when sons and daughters are restored.

# Chapter 5: Nuclear Fusion

## *Restoring the Power of Family Relationships*

We have been given the picture of what marriage and family was supposed to look like, as created by a loving Father in the garden. Now, we also understand that it was the separation from the Father, by sin, that took us out of relationship with our Daddy and brought enmity between relationships and all of creation. Because of Jesus, we can once again have a restored relationship with our Papa God. Jesus became enmity for us and brought restoration to the world, so that once again, our relationships can be restored.

Overcoming the orphan spirit not only brings freedom from bondage in our lives, but it also restores the platform upon which all of our family relationships can be restored. Once these relationships are restored, then family can once again fulfill its destiny in subduing the earth for His kingdom.

The Claussen family ministry is not just that of teaching but of testimony. We are living and experiencing every day the transformational power of identity. Personally, I had a breakthrough in my marriage that I did not see prior to understanding who I am in the Father's love. My wife's radical testimony of being apprehended and overwhelmed by her Father's unconditional love over her actually has changed the culture in our home. Our children are able to ride the wave of family purpose and destiny, rather than having to create their own wave. This allows freedom and peace in our home, and our kids are free to just be kids.

It is from this place of testimony that I release this vision to you of what home can look like when centered on the understanding that we are sons and daughters.

# The Core Has Been Restored

I would like to go back to Jack, our orphaned man, used as an example in chapter 3. Let's examine how things would look different if Jack and Jill embrace the Father's love and displace the orphan spirit.

Jack acknowledges his orphan state. Even though he is a Christian and has received Jesus as his Savior, he has the revelation that he is "dancing at the door" and has not fully received the very message of Jesus. Jesus came to declare the Father to Jack and to restore and fill the very thing that is missing in his life.

Jack realizes that his past experiences and his own natural parents shaped his view of his heavenly Father. He understands that the hurt and pain of childhood was not the way the Father intended it to be. He understands that his natural father was uncomfortable with love and chose not to express that love to him. Because this was not modeled in his own life, Jack, too, became uncomfortable with love. He used to be very comfortable with Jesus as his Savior, his rescuer, but the notion of a loving, affectionate Father was foreign to him. With this knowledge and revelation, he is able to forgive his parents and be healed of the hurt and rejection in his own life.

The Father also reveals to Jack His true countenance over him. Jack quickly learns that the heavenly Father is safe and loving. His Daddy smiles over him, is pleased with him, and has a happy countenance over him. He learns of his worth, acceptance, and inheritance as a son of the Most High God. Most important, Jack begins to have encounters with the loving presence of his Father. He is able to hear his Daddy's voice, because he is no longer an orphan but a son. He regularly receives waves of love and experiential encounters with the Father. His identity becomes secure, and he is able to detect and resist the lies of the Enemy.

# One Flesh

The Father revealed to me that orphans pivot. They are generally immovable and have one foot planted, while the other foot spins around in search of anyone who can meet their need. He explained to me that sons and daughters run. Because they hear their Daddy's voice, they can receive their purpose and run toward that purpose with power.

Jack begins to run. He runs with pleasure, and his eyes are fixed on his Daddy. He realizes that running for His kingdom isn't always easy, but it is peaceful and joyful, because he is in the center of what the Father has for him. Instead of pivoting and looking for someone to meet his need, he simply runs. As he runs, however, the Holy Spirit turns his head, and he notices a young lady running next to him. Jill, too, has her identity secured, and they find that they are running in the same direction. He is drawn and attracted to her, not because of the orphan need within him but because of the way she runs. They see a strength in running together. They feel the Father's pleasure and the providence of their finding each other on their journey. They fall in love for all the right reasons.

Because of the condition of their hearts, fully complete by the presence of a loving God, their love for each other is the *fruit*, not the *fuel*. Their love for each other does not have to be "good enough" to meet the other's need, which was never theirs to carry for each other in the first place. Instead, their love for each other can simply be the outflow, the overflow of who they are as sons and daughters. Their love for each other can build up and promote, rather than be a temporary balm to their hurting hearts and lack of worth.

Jack and Jill become one flesh in marriage. They understand that they aren't two complementary pieces of a puzzle or that they "complete one another," but they become one flesh. This is not intimidating to them at all because of the revelation that when one is promoted, they both are promoted. When one hurts, they both hurt. An orphan is inwardly focused and becomes intimidated by another's greatness. When a marriage is defined with secure identities, then the marriage is defined with sacrificial service and words of encouragement. Their marriage is defined by unity.

This couple secured their identity prior to becoming married, and now they run as one. They have a double portion through covenant—all that he has, in addition to all that she has. Marriage will be the most important human life decision that they will ever make—not just for their future joy and happiness, but because it will be the starting point, the launching pad, for the most important societal entity ever created: the family. Because they are both hearing Daddy's voice, they can have a unified vision for their family. They not only have the answer to *if* they will have children but *why* they want to have children.

# The Father's Voice

*The goal in raising sons and daughters is to raise sons and daughters.* That is why we are to be fruitful and multiply—to spread the culture of the garden over the rest of the world. Once again, this is done through family. There is something supernatural in family. It is God-ordained and God-chosen. You don't get to choose your parents. Parents were meant to be the natural and spiritual protectors for their children. Even though many have set down that mandate, it doesn't change the mandate! Others can come into your life and fulfill some of the mandate, but I want to be clear: that isn't the Father's original, perfect plan.

It is time for natural parents to step into their full destiny, as intended by the Father from the beginning of time. Our desire to have children or to adopt a child should come from the destiny that is on our family. Healthy, secure marriages with a vision for family is a giant step toward restoration.

Jack and Jill understand who they are; they are unified in marriage, and from this place, they have a vision for children. They move into the exhilarating and humbling world of parenting. Because they are comfortable with love, it is easily released and expressed in their home toward each other and their children. The generational cycle of hurt and abuse, guilt and shame, and unattainable expectations is broken. In just one generation, where Daddy's love has brought restoration, generations of dysfunction are overcome. The freedom from bondage found in one generation will be inherited in the next.

A general understanding of Christianity is that after children are born, they will need to be born again. Scripture is clear that everyone needs the saving knowledge of Christ in their own lives. It is the parents' responsibility to introduce the children to the Door, so that they may become born again through the saving blood of Jesus. What is often missed is that the Door is *just the beginning*. We need to explain to our children that a door is to be walked through, and we need to release them into the exciting adventure that is the kingdom.

What happens next is that children become familiar with the Father's voice. Just like the newborn baby who recognizes its mother's voice at birth, so it is with our children at a young age when they receive their heavenly Father's love. Just as they listen to your voice, they can be taught to listen to the Father's voice, and it is our job as parents to help them steward that ability.

For example, if an older brother asks a younger brother, "What did Dad say we should do?" The younger brother may say, "He said to go outside and play football." The older brother would confirm that this sounds like something Dad would say. If he asked the younger brother, "Where did Dad say we should play?" and the younger brother answered, "He said to play in the middle of a busy freeway," the older brother then would sense that this was not something that Dad would say and that the younger brother should go back to Daddy and ask him again. In a similar manner, as your children get older, parents can begin to instruct them to go ask their heavenly Father answers to their questions and then bring those answers back to the parents. The discerning parents can then confirm with the children whether they are hearing the voice of God, correctly and clearly. This is a wonderful way to transfer children's dependence on hearing your voice to hearing the Father's voice.

*The ultimate goal for our children is to hear the Father's voice for themselves.* The Father's voice is always pure and always has perfect motives. The orphan spirit can be overcome at an early age, so the devastating effects, baggage, and wounding can be avoided. The goal should never be to raise independent children. There should simply be a transfer of dependence, from when they are babies, requiring everything from their natural parents, to when they leave your home, completely dependent on the Father's voice. Parents have the unique responsibility to first *display* the Father's love, then to *introduce* the Father's love, and then to *release* their children into the Father's love.

# Intentional Parenting

We need to change the culture from passive parenting to intentional parenting. We need to be intentional in letting our children know the destiny on our family. We need to dream and talk out loud in front of our children. We need to let them know that they belong to something greater than themselves. It is this culture that overcomes an independent, narcissistic mind-set, which is way too prevalent in our young people and in society today. This overcoming culture is found in strong families who understand their destiny.

Jack and Jill have vision and destiny. They realize that all the hard work, sacrifice, and dedication it takes to raise a family is worth it and is part of the master plan for their family on earth. Working hard, balancing the checkbook, doing laundry, changing dirty diapers, changing the sheets at 3:00 a.m. after their child threw up—it is all worship.

Any way that you sow into your family is kingdom. Words of encouragement toward your spouse, taking time to hear your children's stories, and playing football with them in the backyard are all a glorious demonstration of the Father's kingdom.

Just being family is the point. As stated before, the kingdom isn't always easy, but families go through life together—the good times and the bad times—and this is what makes families strong. Strong families are what this world needs so desperately.

Jack and Jill will go through difficulties like all families do. They will face financial hardships, sicknesses, arguments, and conflicts. They know that their family has life and destiny and that they are not to live in enmity. They treat these conflicts as countercultural. They learn to keep short accounts, be very quick to forgive, and exercise consistent discipline to promote godly character.

Because they are secure in their identity, they are generous and giving and are able to sow into other families and their local church. Others are drawn to them, and their home is the place other kids like to hang out. This is true because the other children feel the spirit of life and peace on their home.

# Family Context

Jack and Jill create context for their children. Even when the children are older and leave the home, they never leave the context. The family destiny and spirit continues on for the generations that follow. The cycle of sons and daughters then continues to the next generation. Their children don't run from the family because they are carrying too much weight. Rather, they are sent from the family to go subdue what belongs to them. They don't leave to escape their parents' control; rather, they leave to fulfill their family's destiny.

There is a difference between fathering and controlling. When we control others, the best that we can hope for is for them to look like us. Our ceiling becomes their ceiling. The children feel the pressure, and the parents feel the disappointment when that ceiling is not met. Control is based on fear, insecurity, and performance. It is orphan at its core. Control has our own best interest in mind so that we don't become disappointed, or worse, it keeps our children from surpassing us, which would only expose our own insecurities and low self-worth.

Fathers look to promote their children. *The father's ceiling becomes his children's floor.* When parents are secure in their identity and destiny for their family, their children simply get to walk in inheritance of everything that has already been built. They don't have to bear the weight of meeting the needs of their parents. They simply get to build their own destiny upon that which the parents and the generations that came before have already built. The parents, of course, are still needed from a structural standpoint, much as a fourteenth floor would need a thirteenth floor.

The children aren't expected to just build whatever they want. They build within the context of the family. The only difference is that it is higher, it is promoted, and it is greater.

When we correct or discipline our children in the context of parenting, it is always to bring promotion, never shame. It should always be to build up, never to break down.

# Parenting Is for Parents

Parents need to honor the assignment. No one else on the face of the earth can provide everything that your children need better than you can. This is the way that God ordained it to be. Everything that you need to raise your children is contained within you. Unfortunately, parents have become disenfranchised and intimidated. They have become impotent and negligent. For too long, society has told parents that they are unqualified. Yet the responsibility for parenting cannot be divvied up to day care providers, schoolteachers, or youth pastors and certainly not to children's peers. Parenting is for parents.

Families in our society have become weak, because parents have allowed them to become weak. Our children were never intended to have us as their buddies, their advisors, their mentors, their drill sergeants, or even their friends … but we were meant to be their parents. There is no other word or relationship like it. There is no other relationship that carries the same weight and responsibility.

Jack and Jill have embraced their role as parents. They have put loving boundaries around their children and have created a peaceful, joyful home. They work every day to steward their identity as sons and daughters, because they know the Enemy will always attack us at the level of our identity. They work every day to steward their marriage relationship. They make sure they are always working toward each other and never away from each other. They work every day to steward their relationship with their children. They speak life and love to them every day. They offer them freedom within the context of loving boundaries, and they train them to hear the voice of their Daddy God.

You cannot control other people's relationship with the heavenly Father. Your responsibility is your own heart. However, when you allow the extravagant love of the Father to wash over you, it will change your perspective on every relationship that you are in. It is the Spirit of the Son that cries out within you, "Abba Father," and it is the Spirit of the Son that declares the Father to an orphan world. I promise you this: if you allow the Spirit to shine through your life, it will be contagious.

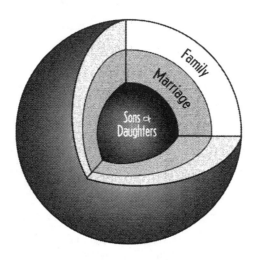

When sons and daughters are at the core of our concentric circle example, then marriages and family become the nucleus of society. If you agree with the premise that family is powerful, then you must do everything in your power to restore family relationships. Just as with nuclear fusion, the power of the nuclear family will be determined by the strength of the bonds in the family.

Once we are satisfied and secure in our identity today, we can then be brave and courageous to start dealing with the things in our past. Our family ancestors who have gone before us have treasures that are available for us. To be fully equipped to subdue the earth, we need to possess everything that belongs to our family. In the next chapter, we will explore the power of inheritance.

# Chapter 6: Power Generation

## *Restoring the Power of Family Inheritance*

We now have the full understanding of how important family is and a vision for how it originally looked. Our identity is now secured; which brings healing and restoration to our family relationships, so we can set our sights on what family was originally created to do: subdue the earth. However, there is still one more tool that will help us become even more prepared and equipped for the task for which we were created. That tool is inheritance.

In many respects, inheritance is the easiest way to receive. By definition, inheritance is receiving something that you didn't earn. We can receive a gift, an award, a wage. We can receive through favor, and through impartation, but all of these are somewhat dependent on our ability or our participation. Inheritance, on the other hand, is simply given to us because of our position as a son or daughter. Once again, our identity and our position is of utmost importance.

When we struggle with an orphan spirit and feel separated from the Father, we often lose sight of, and miss our inheritance. Similarly, when we are raised in a harmful or hurtful environment, we tend to disconnect ourselves, not only from the painful relationships but also from the inheritance that is afforded to us through family.

In this chapter, I will discuss two aspects of our inheritance. We will explore our spiritual inheritance as sons and daughters of the Most High God and what was afforded to us when Jesus, our co-laborer, restored our identity and authority. You will discover why it is important to go after your natural inheritance from your earthly parents and the generations that preceded them. Furthermore, you will understand the importance of living with the generational mind-set of the legacy you will leave your children as an inheritance.

# Heirs of God

Clearly, in no way could we earn or even qualify for our inheritance as sons and daughters of the Most High God. It was unmistakably an act of one man, Jesus, who shed his blood to make that possible. Because of Jesus and the Spirit of adoption, we have been welcomed back by the Father, and by His overwhelming grace, our inheritance has been restored.

"For you did not receive the spirit of bondage again to fear, but you received the Spirit of adoption by whom we cry out, Abba, Father. The Spirit Himself bears witness with our spirit that we are children of God, and if children, then heirs—*heirs of God and joint heirs with Christ*, if indeed we suffer with Him, that we may also be glorified together (Romans 8:15–17, italics added).

"But when the fullness of time had come, God sent forth His Son, born of a woman, born under the law, to redeem those who were under the law that we might receive the adoption as sons. And because you are sons, God has sent forth the Spirit of His Son into your hearts, crying out, Abba Father. Therefore you are no longer a slave but a son, and if a son, then *an heir of God through Christ* (Galatians 4:4–7, italics added).

It also says in Ephesians 1:11–14 that the Holy Spirit has sealed us (with authority) and is the guarantee of our inheritance.

Scripture is crystal clear that when we accept Christ, we have the right to be called children. When we exercise that right and fully understand our identity, then we are heirs, and so begins the radical life of living with full access to the kingdom. We have inherited all of heaven. *We have been sealed with His Spirit and given the family name.*

It all comes back to identity. Once we know who we are and whose we are, all of life looks different. Unless we allow the Father's love to displace our orphan spirit, we will continue to feel unqualified, unloved, impotent, and out of place. Spiritual orphans have no legal right to the inheritance. To pass on to our natural children the immense power of inheritance we need to fully embrace the inheritance afforded to us through our loving Father. We, as parents, get to demonstrate to our children the fullness and the completeness found in the relationship with our Daddy God. Part of that completeness is understanding what is ours through inheritance.

# Asking for What We Already Have

Returning to the prodigal son story, even though I feel the story is about the father, we can learn from the two sons. Both of these sons had an orphan spirit and did not fully understand their inheritance.

The younger son manifested the orphan spirit, bondage by the seduction of sin, and the independent spirit. He felt there was greater freedom when he was out from under the father's house. He wanted freedom to seek his own satisfaction, but in the end, he came into shame and bondage. He needed to understand that even though there were boundaries in his own home, it was there that he could operate in complete freedom and have access to all his father possessed.

The older son was also an orphan. The older son exemplified the orphan spirit by performance and a servant mentality. Performance deceives the orphan spirit into striving to earn what it already possesses through inheritance. The older son was waiting for his father to reward his performance. The son could have walked in and taken whatever he wanted without having to work for it. Instead, he worked in some far-off corner of the farm, when he could have been with the father. Orphans judge others and live with an unfulfilled sense of entitlement. He went insane with envy, jealousy, and anger when that wicked son came back, and Dad threw him a party. He could not handle someone receiving freely what he worked so hard for and still did not have.

Orphans tend to ask and plead for what they already have. Sons understand their inheritance and ask for counsel from the Father on how best to use it. When we approach the Father as a son, we approach Him differently than as a slave. When we have been given authority and inheritance, the Father expects us to use it. It affects how we pray, how we read Scripture, and even how we listen to His voice.

Even when Jesus taught us how to pray, He had us address the Father with declaration and authority. He told us to pray with the goal of having earth look like heaven. He instructed us to pray declarations that would back up that goal: give us, forgive us, lead us, and deliver us. If we pray from the spirit of bondage, we will find ourselves asking and pleading—and ultimately, groveling and complaining.

An orphan who is entitled looks different from a son with authority. An orphan will approach the throne timidly and will invoke the law and self-empowerment in an attempt to sway or plead with his Master. A son will approach the throne with authority and will invoke grace and service in an attempt to improve his Father's kingdom here on earth.

A son also reads the Bible differently. As stated in Romans 8, we are no longer under the spirit of bondage but the Spirit of the Son. When we read Scripture from the Spirit of a son, it is as if we are reading our inheritance. We don't get bogged down in all the things that we are supposed to do and what we are doing wrong; rather, we discover who He is, what we can do for Him, and what He can do through us.

# Heavenly Secrets

When a son has been washed and baptized in the love of the Father, he is unafraid to sit on his Daddy's lap and listen. The Father talks to us as a Father would talk to His son. There is intimacy and compassion in His voice. He is for us, not against us. He is joyful over us, not angry with us. When we position ourselves on His lap, He will tell us secrets. He hasn't kept the secrets *from* us; He has kept these secrets *for* us. An orphan will be crushed under the weight and responsibility of knowing the secret things on the Father's heart, so He has held these secrets for sons and daughters, because they will not only embrace the secret things but can implement them from a place of rest.

John 15:15 explains that the Father does not reveal secrets to slaves. Slaves do not understand or know what the Master is doing.

"The secret things belong to the Lord our God, but those things which are revealed belong to us and to our children forever ..." (Deuteronomy 29:29).

My testimony is a journey from an orphan mind-set to an inheritance mind-set. As mentioned in the beginning of this book, I was raised in a very loving family. My mother and father demonstrated very well the loving heart of the Father. I never went to bed at night, wondering if I was loved. I never lived in fear of damaging words or other abuses. Because of this, understanding the Father's love was never difficult for me. However, understanding and experiencing are two different things.

I was a high achiever. Whether it was academics or sports I always pushed myself to be the best—or one of the best. This desire to achieve would be strengthened by the accolades and acknowledgments that I would get from others, including my parents. I migrated toward difficult endeavors, such as medical school and running marathons. I felt these things would set me apart and would clearly pad my sense of worth and my quest for admiration. It is easy to imagine, then, how I assumed that if I could perform well for my heavenly Father, I would receive His admiration as well.

I really loved the Lord. I would operate in the gifts of the Holy Spirit, and I was compelled by the dynamic speakers and kingdom messages. I was so moved and compelled that I would dream of being able to deliver those messages myself. I was convinced that I had the ability to speak and preach, and if I didn't, I would just have to work harder to achieve that dream. I would observe and emulate the popular speakers. I would study their style and mannerisms, knowing that if I ever was given the opportunity, I could be just like they were. I admired them, but in my heart, I actually was jealous of them. I wasn't accustomed to being on the sidelines.

Ironically, the Lord gave me a platform when the pastor at my church invited me to preach on occasion. This exercise forced me to talk to God about what I was to say, and He led me to study certain Scriptures to give foundation to my messages. In this way, I went down the road of a significant transition and shifting in my life. Through Scripture, the Lord revealed to me that when I accepted Christ, I actually died. It is no longer I who live, but Christ lives in me (Galatians 2:20). Scripture is also clear that since I died with Him, I also rose with Him. I was a new creation, living a resurrected life. This meant to me, in no uncertain terms, that my life was not my own.

I began a journey of sonship. I was able to strengthen my relationship with my loving Father, and He gently and lovingly walked me through a season of surrender. I would literally walk around the fields on our acreage and lay down all the things that I worked so hard to build up. The Father wasn't interested in my achievements. He was only interested in me. So during those walks, I laid down all my dreams and lofty aspirations and told my Daddy that I was satisfied with whatever He gave me. As long as I was eating at His table, I would be satisfied.

Prior to this, I had been running hard for the Lord, and had put many things on my table. I was busy doing good things, declaring truth, establishing relationships, and ministering with passion. I was feeling tired and somewhat worn out, but that just meant I was working hard for the Lord. After this new revelation of the Father's love in my life, in conjunction with my observing this new love of the Father in my wife's life, I started focusing on *being* rather than *doing*. I was a son of the Most High God, and in that, I was completely satisfied. If all He asked me to do was to be a husband to my wife and a father to my children, I would become content in that.

So one day, I grabbed my notebook, sat down with the Lord, and asked him a life-changing question. I asked, "What is mine to carry?" Although I was doing a lot of things that were *good*, I needed to know what was *mine*. He only told me two or three things, with the surprising instruction to play board games with my kids. That might not have been the world-changing instruction I was hoping for, but I obeyed. This started the season in our home of "hunkering down." I set down many of the previous responsibilities, and we began a season of just "doing family."

Interestingly, while I was basking in my Daddy's love for me and the revelation that I didn't have to earn it, my heavenly Father began to talk to me as a son. A slave doesn't know what his master is doing. When I was able to set down my prideful, self-oriented agenda and just sit on my Papa's lap and listen to His heart, He told me secrets.

I entered into a wild and crazy season of rapid revelation and downloads of information. I wouldn't go anywhere without my notebook, knowing that in any circumstance or any time of day or night, He might speak to me secrets of His kingdom and, more specifically, about family. I would wake up in the middle of the night with fresh revelation and frequently have a "working breakfast" with my wife and children, explaining to them what the Lord revealed to me through the night. I would hop on my riding lawn mower, with questions prepared to ask the Lord while I mowed the lawn. I would be amazed when He consistently answered. (Much of this book was written from "lawn mower revelation.") As I was living a simplistic life, just enjoying my family (playing board games), He was revealing to me the kingdom implications of what I was doing.

There did come a time when this message would be shared and now, ironically, I do have a platform to tell others about His kingdom and about family. The Lord knew that some things had to break off me. My orphan spirit needed to be displaced by His love, so that I could deliver His message for His kingdom, not for my worth. I realized that I didn't need to be like other speakers, I could just be me. I understand now that the gift of this message can be shared because of my inheritance as a son. First position, then purpose, and then power. I can testify that I'm now living a life with purpose and power, but it wasn't given to me until I found my identity. The Father's secrets weren't told to me until I understood my inheritance.

# Desires of Your Heart

The Lord gave me the desire of my heart, in His perfect timing, for the right reasons. The word desire means "from the Father." It says in Psalm 37:4–5, "Delight yourself also in the Lord, and He shall give you the desires of your heart. Commit your way to the Lord, trust also in Him, and He shall bring it to pass."

I believe this does not mean we have desires in our hearts, and we hope that He blesses them. I think it means that we have desires in our hearts, and He birthed them. He put the desire there; it is from the Father. He is interested in and cares about what is on our hearts, and He opens all of heaven to us as an inheritance. He is the Creator of creativity, design, invention, dreams, and visions. It is noble to have a soldier mentality, where we just receive marching orders and do His work, but *He is more interested in a son who is nobility than a soldier who is noble.* It is very possible that the Father who gives good gifts is the very author of the desire that is in your heart, and He will back you with all of heaven because of inheritance.

It is the inheritance mind-set that listens to the Father's voice and runs with joy. He has given each of us part of this world to subdue, and when we are heirs with Christ, nothing is impossible. It is the inheritance mind-set that runs toward the adventure, knowing that it might not be easy, but it is from Daddy. It is the inheritance mind-set that doesn't ask for what he already has.

I would venture to say that this world does not hold enough years to fully understand what it means to inherit all of heaven. It is way beyond what I can fathom, but I am determined, in my lifetime, to inherit all that I can as a beloved son.

# What's in a Name?

It will require the same tenacity and determination to inherit everything we can from our natural families and generations. Although the inheritance that is offered to us from our natural family pales in comparison to what is offered to us from our heavenly family, it is no less important. It is critical to the restoration of family—and thus, the restoration of the world—that we receive all of our rightful inheritance. We must see the value and importance in our earthly heritage in order to take back what the Enemy may have stolen.

There is little doubt in the significance of our family names. Certainly, there is historical, cultural, and regional significance in our actual names. Oftentimes, our surnames will be a direct reflection of our fathers. The most obvious and common example would be an English surname such as Johnson (son of John) or Wilson (son of William). My last name most likely is a Danish or German derivation—Claussen, son of Claus. The Hebrew tradition uses bin or ben. An example of this would be Judah Ben-Hur, from Hollywood fame, or Benjamin, which means son of a right-hand man. Other cultures have familiar examples, using, for example, Mac or Mc—McDonald being son of Donald—or ski in Polish or Russian, such as Michalski as the son of Michael. Even just the addition of the letter S to the last name indicates sonship, such as Edwards, the son of Edward. These names would serve not only as identification but also would have meaning in the region and neighborhood as to the integrity and significance of the father's name.

I realize that our names and even our last names may have lost significance in our society, but I feel that this needs to be restored. Again, because of hurt and pain that may have occurred in our family lines, we often don't look at our names through a lens of integrity, hope, and joy. Yet we need to understand that it wasn't intended to be that way. God is a God of restoration, and I believe in this time and in our generation, He is restoring family names, inheritances, and heritages.

# Family History

As subduers of the earth, we need to rise up and take back what rightfully belongs to us. We need to "footstool," or subdue, the things that have been given to us. Our family histories cannot be changed, but they can be restored and subdued. As sons and daughters of the Most High God, we are not subject to our histories but only to our destinies. We, however, do have a family destiny that was imparted into our family lines from the beginning of time by the loving hand of a covenant-keeping God. Even though we may have had generations in our family lines that turned away from the Father's perfect plan, we now have authority to receive everything that rightfully belongs to us through inheritance.

When I see a patient in the emergency department or clinic, a critical piece of information that I try to obtain is a family history. A family history will often shed light on some generational predispositions toward disease and sickness. Often, based on family history, I may implement certain screening tests and preventive measures and may even implement treatment to prevent and combat these risk factors.

For instance, if you have a family history of diabetes, your risk for getting diabetes yourself will certainly be much higher than someone who does not have that family history. You can stand against it, rebuke it, or cast it out, but the fact is, it doesn't remove the history of diabetes in your family line. We, however, do have authority over it. I feel that we are not obligated to accept it or live in fear of it. Our bodies should be subdued, and the Enemy would have us think that we are powerless and subject to those forces of evil and sickness that have plagued our generations. That is a lie. For too long, the Enemy has had a stranglehold on family generations. Let's be clear; the Enemy is defeated. He is a withering branch cut off from its life source. He had his authority removed by the blood of Jesus. The only way that he can be empowered is if we allow him to be, through our negligence and fear.

Not only do we have physical illness and sickness in our family lines, but we also have generational curses, mind-sets, and sins. In your family line, you may have generational issues with anger, abuse, alcoholism, abandonment, divorce, mental illness, stoicism—the list goes on and on. Please remember, however, that these were not present in the garden. These things were never part of God's original plan. Sin and rebellion have consequences, and you, through your family, may be a victim of those consequences. We are no longer under the "spirit of bondage again to fear, but we have received the Spirit of adoption." I believe that our family histories and generational issues can be healed, covered, and restored through Jesus' blood and our identity as sons and daughters. I believe that the fear of these issues can be wiped away as we gaze into the Father's loving eyes.

# Value the Birthright

We need to have a certain tenacity for our rightful birthright. We must look past the way things are, to where things should be. Before we can subdue the earth, we must first subdue what belongs to us. In order for our families to be fully equipped to subdue the earth, we must possess everything that belongs to us through inheritance.

A great example of this tenacity for inheritance is found in the story of Jacob and Esau. In Genesis, chapters 25 and 27, we're told the story of the twin sons of Isaac. Esau was the older son, born first by a matter of minutes, but with his younger brother holding onto his heel. Jacob had prophetic destiny on his life, as his mother was told, "The older shall serve the younger."

Jacob possessed a hunger and a value for the covenant and birthright that was upon his family. According to the custom in the area, a man could sell his birthright to his brother. The birthright meant headship of the family and a double share of the inheritance. Because of direct revelation from the Lord, Rebekah and Jacob understood the importance of the birthright and the blessing. Because of the zeal for his family inheritance, Jacob took what was not his and made it his reality. Conversely, Esau had no value for his birthright and sold what was rightfully his.

> Now Jacob cooked a stew; and Esau came in from the field, and was weary. And Esau said to Jacob, please feed me with that same red stew for I am weary. Therefore his name was called Edom. But Jacob said, sell me your birthright as of this day. And Esau said look, I'm about to die; so what is this birthright to me? Then Jacob said, swear to me as of this day. So he swore to him, and sold his birthright to Jacob and Jacob gave Esau bread and stew of lentils; that he ate and drank, arose, and went his way. Thus Esau despised his birthright. (Genesis 25:29–34)

Jacob's tactics were certainly questionable. It is possible that one could interpret Esau as a victim. However, despite

Jacob's use of deception to obtain the birthright and later the blessing, God's interpretation of the matter is surprising. The Lord didn't punish the deceiver and restore the victim. He chose the one who valued the birthright and rejected the one who despised it. Romans 9:13 says, "Jacob I have chosen but Esau I have rejected." Jacob didn't accept his history but instead pursued his destiny. He had a tenacity and a value for what was spoken over his family, and he wanted the entirety for himself, even to a double portion. Because of this, the Father knew this was someone upon whom He could build a nation.

I believe every family has a destiny, and every family can offer an inheritance. When the leaders of a family realize that they are building a foundation for generations, even something they may never see in their lifetimes; when they lead with tenacity and take everything that belongs to them; when they pursue things that are not their reality and make them their reality, then they set up an inheritance mind-set that will be present for generations.

I believe there is still a double portion for my children, which is simply all that they have, built upon all that I have. As previously mentioned, my ceiling becomes their floor. We need to get the picture that families are structures that are erected one floor on top of the other. Families are to be generational, where we value the floors beneath us and provide the floors that will be built above us.

My parents have provided a solid floor for me to build upon. I am aware that it came at a price. I am fully aware and grateful for the generations that have come before me and have come to the conclusion that I can receive everything from them. Whether it was stewarded well or not, it is rightfully mine. I do not, however, have to receive any bondage or generational sin that may have been present in my heritage.

One day, I asked my father and mother to lay hands on me and bless me. Just as Isaac did for Jacob, I asked that everything that they carry would be imparted to me. I fully understand that my family story doesn't begin with me, and I'm even more certain that it doesn't end with me. I am truly blessed, and I value the foundations that have been laid for me, for my family, and for my future generations.

# The Ground Floor

I do understand that many who read this book may feel that they do not have a godly inheritance. All you may have inherited is pain. Then, you need to realize the importance of a ground floor. You have the unique position to obtain something that I will never be able to obtain. You will be the start of something great. It will come with a price, but what is built upon you will be magnificent. Just as I honor my parents for laying a godly foundation for me to build upon, your children will look upon you with the same honor and admiration. This is the tenacity that I'm passionate about. We, as families, need to have a vision for something beyond ourselves. This is the mind-set that will bring transformation across the earth in a matter of generations.

Let me explain to you the price that you need to pay. This process will require you to reexamine relationships that may have been too painful to look at. The relationships in your family, past and present, are worth restoring. This is an important revelation. *Everything you need from your parents is contained within your parents.* Everything you need from your grandparents is contained within your grandparents. You may not have realized this, and they may not have realized this, but remember, when God set His plan for the earth, it was set—unmovable. Even though your ancestors may not have fully appreciated their identity as sons and daughters, they still were given something for you. This is how the Father intended it to be. I am asking you to be willing, within your ability, to pursue reconciliation and restoration with your family members. There will be a price, but it is worth it.

It is worth it, because there is something for you contained within the process of restoration. It is worth it, because your newfound identity as a son or daughter of the Most High God is contagious. The very security and presence of a loving Father within you will change the atmosphere over you and your family, just as you enter the room. It is worth it, because you will be empowered as one with authority on the earth to take back what the enemy has stolen. It is worth it, because when you are no longer an orphan, you will no longer require something from these relationships that was never theirs to give.

If you feel the tenacity burning within you to reexamine some of these relationships from which you may have walked away, either literally or emotionally, let me provide you a few guidelines. First, deal with unforgiveness toward yourself. This will allow you then to be armed only with love. Only His love within you can turn a heart of stone to a heart of flesh. It will be your unconditional love and testimony that will bring transformation in your family.

Second, don't go to your family as an orphan. (Don't move past identity!) Make sure your identity is secure, or the same feelings and issues will instantly rise up within you and, once again, your needs will not be met. Third, make sure your attempt at reconciliation is within the confines of safety for you and your family. Not every situation is restorable in its current state. If these relationships are overtly abusive or in any way would threaten your safety, then you need to talk to your heavenly Father and trusted mentors for an effective strategy. No one is out of reach of the loving hand of God. In this situation, I still would urge you not to give up, but certainly exercise wisdom. Last, and perhaps the most difficult, don't initially expect anything in return. You cannot approach reconciliation feeling like you are owed something. With your newfound identity, ask the loving Father to displace any unforgiveness that is within you toward them. Approach your family with their debts already forgiven.

# Generational Restoration

I believe with all my heart that family restoration is what the Lord is doing right now across the earth. The ministry of family restoration is a healing ministry in a very real way. If this generation will rise up and pursue healing for their families and across generations, I believe the fullness of inheritance then will be realized. I believe that a great percentage of sickness and disease will fall away, because so much of our physical ailments are rooted in spiritual and generational oppression.

We cannot despise our birthright. Jesus' blood offered us so much more than just salvation. It offered us healing and restoration, and family is in the center of his restoration plan. It has to be!

Let's return to Jack and Jill. As mentioned before, Jack's relationship with his father was strained. Throughout the generations, the men in Jack's family had difficulty showing and relating emotion. Jack's dad was uncomfortable with love. He definitely was uncomfortable demonstrating his love to his wife and children. This created a hurt and separation within the home, with Jack always feeling like he had to perform for his father's admiration and attention. Jack's journey toward sonship with his loving heavenly Father brought healing to that empty place he had in his heart. As he became more comfortable with his identity, he began to feel the importance of family, not only for his own marriage and children but for the generations that came before and the generations that would follow. Jack knew there was something locked within his father that needed to be released. Through intentional ministry and time in the Father's presence, Jack was able to forgive his father, and his anger was turned into compassion. He also repented of the rebellious spirit he had toward his parents and his willingness to harbor bitterness.

Jack became more intentional in his relationship with his father. He made sure to include his father in family activities and tried to connect with him over the phone. When ending his phone conversations, Jack told his dad that he loved him. At first, his dad would just respond with "okay," but every once in a while, Jack would receive a "you too." The real breakthrough occurred, however, when one day, Jack's dad responded with "I love you too." To Jack, it was as if a gigantic generational wall had come crashing down, and nothing has been the same for their family since then.

The relationship between Jack's parents also began to improve as his dad became more comfortable with love toward his wife. Jack's mom had also suffered from rejection, depression, and anger over the years. Jack always loved and respected his mother but kept her at a safe distance and remained emotionally removed. Jack became intentional to unconditionally love his mother and to include her in his family. He often asked her advice in the raising of their children. She felt honored and accepted by Jack and Jill and the grandchildren. She asked Jack and Jill more about the Lord and the security of their identity as His son and daughter. She realized that she was dependent on affirmation from her husband for her worth, and when she didn't get it, she felt worthless. Even at an advanced age, Jack's parents began a journey through the door into the Father's embrace. Jack, in turn, felt the gravity and importance of a foundation laid by his parents and a greater discovery of his inheritance.

## Spiritual Mothers and Fathers

Jill's testimony as a young girl also was painful. Her parents divorced when she was quite young, and she never knew her father. Her understanding of fatherhood was clouded by a spirit of abandonment and rejection. Her mother did the best she could to raise a young girl on her own but unfortunately found an escape in drugs and alcohol. Jill, as a teenager, found her worth and identity in her social circles. She found some acceptance by her peers but her life was one of rebellion, drugs, and promiscuity. When Jill was in her early twenties, her mother died from complications of a drug overdose, and Jill truly felt alone. Finally, at the end of her rope, she sought help. She entered rehab, but more important, she found Jesus. The blood of Jesus washed her clean from all her sins and restored her life. Despite her newfound salvation, she had no real understanding of a loving Father. As she attended church, several well-intentioned people offered to be her "spiritual mother and father," but as Jill's needs mounted, these people often backed away, which only added to Jill's orphan issues. However, one couple understood what it meant to be a spiritual mother and father. They felt from the Lord to invite Jill into their family and to demonstrate to her the love of the Father and to offer her a godly inheritance.

For this family movement to be successful, I believe it requires true spiritual mothers and fathers. However, we need to be very clear on what this means. I want to be crystal clear that I believe our natural parents should be our spiritual fathers and mothers. This is what the Father originally intended, and we should do everything in our power to restore that relationship. Again, I believe everything that we need from parents is contained within our parents. I also understand, however, that there are many circumstances where this is simply not possible. The body of Christ needs to be willing to stand up in the spirit of adoption and allow those with no godly inheritance to be grafted into our families. We need to understand, though, that if someone is seeking a spiritual mother and father from whom to draw inheritance, we must also assume this person is coming from an orphan place. To offer this person spiritual parenting and not deliver just adds another layer of rejection. Family is not always pretty, and as in Jill's example, many backgrounds are not neat and tidy. If we're going to be spiritual mothers and fathers, we need to be fully prepared and committed. The last thing the person needs is another part-time, uncommitted parent.

It is okay to minister to someone who is hurting and alone and try to help him or her. Furthermore, it is okay to feel like you cannot commit to the process of being someone's spiritual mother and father. Then, in my opinion, it is important to simply use a different word. Words like mentor, counselor, advisor, or friend are all completely appropriate and all serve an extremely important function in someone's life.

I would like to be so bold as to submit to you that if you are called to be a spiritual mother and father, do so with full commitment. In every way, it should be considered an adoption. Remember in Romans 8, it is the spirit of adoption that removes bondage. This means being parents and family to the person in every way. It means including him or her in everything that the family does. It means including him or her in family events, vacations, and holidays. It includes heart-to-heart talks and 2:00 a.m. phone calls. The person should be included in every aspect of family inheritance, and yes, that includes your savings account and 401(k).

This is a high calling. This will require sacrifice from all family members. This is the true essence of family, and some of you will be called to share yours with others.

Prior to meeting Jack, Jill was adopted into a loving family when she was a young adult. It was in this relationship that she witnessed how a marriage and family was to operate. She saw firsthand a culture of honor and commitment that can only be demonstrated in the confines of a family. Her whole paradigm of life radically shifted. She now knew what a loving father could be like. She could now read Scripture as a daughter, not as a slave. She became part of a family. She inherited a value for family and received a birthright. From her broken past, she now had a godly inheritance. With her identity secured, the Father placed the desire in her heart for a husband and a family of her own. She now had an inheritance to pass along.

# Redigging the Wells

"Then Isaac departed from there and pitched his tent in the Valley of Gerar, and dwelt there. And Isaac dug again the wells of water which they had dug in the days of Abraham his father, for the Philistines had stopped them up after the death of Abraham. He called them by the names which his father had called them" (Genesis 26:17–18).

There are things in our family that are worth redigging. There may be years of dirt that the Enemy has thrown on top of your "family well" over the generations. I am asking you to consider digging through some of those past hurts, moving in the spirit of forgiveness, and redigging the well. It is time for all of us to value our birthright and to fully understand that our family carries destiny and inheritance. Your family's well has good water; it is time to drink deeply.

Our ultimate goal as families is to subdue the earth. We will be unable to subdue the earth without inheritance *and* influence. We must fully appreciate that a multistory skyscraper is much more noticeable than a single-story rambler. The inheritance mind-set is so vitally important to the building of heritage, not only for our own families but for the whole world to see. It is through inheritance that we have vertical growth. Whether we are the ground floor, or the fifteenth floor, we always need to be aware of our foundation and future generations.

Now that we are armed with secure identity, strong marriages, dynamic families, *and* godly inheritance, in the next chapter we will explore the tremendous power and influence that our restored families have on the earth.

# Chapter 7: Critical Mass

## *Restoring the Power of Family Influence*

We are now fully equipped to fulfill the original mandate. The excitement in life really begins when we have a picture of our roles and tasks on this earth from our Father. Because of His great love for us, He created the earth unsubdued. Jesus restored our authority and purpose as subduers of the earth. Still created in His image, we have restored dominion, and we need to have unmistakable influence to all peoples. Our identity, spirit, and culture; our unity in family; and our godly inheritance from which we can draw will determine our degree of influence.

The garden of Eden was created for two people. They were to tend and cultivate what was given to them, raise their children in their family culture, and then send them out to subdue the earth; to reproduce the culture of the garden over the rest of the earth. They would be well equipped and fully able to be fruitful and multiply, fill the earth, and subdue it.

Once again, the cultural mandate was never canceled. Through grace, we have the exciting opportunity to once again fulfill the task that was originally afforded to us. Our ability to fulfill this task will be directly dependent on our influence.

To illustrate, $E=mc^2$ is the world's most famous and recognizable equation. In very simplistic terms, "m" is mass and "c" is the speed of light (squared). The speed of light is a gigantic number, and it is constant. A small change in mass will equal a large change in energy ("E"). To influence and subdue the earth, Christian families are the "critical mass" required to combine with the gigantic power of the constant almighty Creator (c) to drive the equation and create the energy needed to subdue the earth. In other words, since the Creator (c) is unchanging, the amount of influence (E) released is dependent on mankind (m) filling the earth. This powerfully illustrates the mandate and the importance of every Christian family to be part of the equation.

# No Other Word Like Family

It is vitally important that families not only be restored but that the word "family" be restored and strengthened. In order for families to take their rightful places of influence on the earth, we need to be unified and single-focused on what the word family means. Unfortunately, the word family has become so redefined and diluted that the world has lost the grip and impact of the word's meaning.

In our culture, we see that everything is referred to as family. We have our Monday night football family, our Tuesday night bowling league family, our Wednesday night Bible study family, our Thursday night bingo family, and our Friday night soccer mom family. Most Christians would even admit to belonging to a "church family." The sad truth is that most people truly want these associations to be family. Because of the hurt and disillusionment in their own families, they are desperately hoping that these other relationships can satisfy, in some way, the need for family. The problem is, they can't. These relationships can offer support, companionship, and even love and encouragement, but they cannot deliver family. They simply can't deliver something they were never created to be.

I understand that as Christians, we are all sons and daughters of God, so then in a sense, we are part of God's family. This would make us brothers and sisters in Christ. Church is the gathering of these brothers and sisters, but as stated before, the function of the church is different from the function of the family. It isn't less important or more important; it is just different. When we try to push off the responsibilities of our nuclear family onto the church, the church then does not get to fulfill its destiny for which it was created. Family simply cannot be focused and powerful if all of these other relationships are considered family.

I feel with all my heart that my family is irreplaceable. There is nothing else on the earth that could be family to me. My parents are my spiritual parents. My wife and children are my nuclear family. To call anything else family would feel awkward and out of place. This is the culture change that I feel needs to take place. Even a change in semantics would send a message to our culture that the nuclear family is strong, unique, and powerful. When we refer to our Thursday night softball team as our friends, our fellow employees as colleagues, and our congregation as operating in community or as the body, I feel we set things back into alignment. I feel that this, in turn, will bring a freedom to the other relationships that will not have to carry the burden of being referred to as family. I also hope that this shift will help us focus and see the value in the restoration of our own nuclear family.

# Was Jesus Hostile toward Family?

There is some confusion in the New Testament in regards to how Jesus responded to family. At times, Jesus seemed to have some hostility toward family. On the night Jesus was born, the angels declared "peace on earth," only for Jesus then to declare in Matthew 10:34, "Do not think that I came to bring peace on earth. I did not come to bring peace but a sword. I've come to set the man against his father, a daughter against her mother, and a daughter-in-law against her mother-in-law and a man's enemies will be those of his own household."

We must never lose sight of the fact that Jesus was the Door. Jesus discerned correctly that one of His biggest barriers for those to follow Him was the law, tradition, and family. It would have been very difficult for someone to leave his or her family tradition and follow this unknown carpenter with strange doctrine. There needed to be a separation from the old way, which couldn't save, to the new, one and only Way, which could save. This, without doubt, would create enemies within households. It would be completely counterintuitive, however, to conclude that Jesus came to cancel the authority and power of family. Family was His plan from the very beginning! His goal wasn't to delete the family structure but to restore it into the new covenant with greater power. It wasn't Jesus' life that brought peace on earth; it was His death and resurrection. Jesus was a narrow door, and as Paul pointed out in 1 Corinthians 4:15, there were not many fathers who walked through. I believe that Malachi 4:5–6, the last prophetic declaration of the Old Testament, was an acknowledgement of the shake-up that would occur, as well as a declaration of the restoration culture purchased by the blood of Jesus: "the hearts of the fathers will be restored to the children and the hearts of the children to their fathers!"

While I am extremely confident that Jesus was not hostile toward family, I am equally confident that there is hostility in our culture today. We need to be clear and unified in our response to that hostility. The nuclear family needs to be defined, powerful, and influential, not ill-defined, divided, distracted, and angry.

# The Cement of Society

The very structure of family is to enter all aspects of society to bring influence. In our orphan example, we saw the domino effect, with the hurting orphan at the core, as the center of the concentric circles. We saw how an orphan looked to his marriage and ultimately to his children to meet his needs. When those needs were not met, he turned to the church. This meant the church could not fulfill its function and mandate, which would then obligate government to overreach. We then saw how things could dramatically change when sons and daughters with secure identity were at the core. This created solid marriages and peaceful, dynamic families. It was then that these dynamic families entered and influenced all aspects of society.

The realms of influence in society and in a city are often referred to as the seven pillars of influence. Historically, the seven pillars have been considered: government, family, business, media, education, religion, and arts and entertainment. I believe these are correct—with one gigantic exception. In this picture of the seven pillars, family is just considered one of the pillars. Instead, I believe that family needs to be the substance of all the other six realms. Using the pillars as an example, I feel Jesus would be the base or the foundation of all aspects of society, because He has been given authority in heaven and on earth. Furthermore, I believe family is not just one of the pillars but the very cement or marble of each of the other six pillars. Based on what we've learned about family, it would be preposterous to think that family is just another societal piece. Family is the core, the very essence and structure of each of the other realms of influence in society.

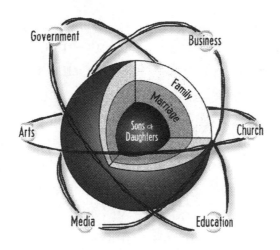

These pillars do give us the picture of how important family is and the realms they need to influence. When families are strong, healthy, and secure, they can then send their family members into businesses, government, and even into church with a service mind-set with the support and backing that only a family can provide. Sending orphans into the realm of media or arts and entertainment often results in disaster. Sending sons and daughters as representatives of secure families into these realms brings clarity, integrity, and a positive cultural transformation.

Our family members are like ambassadors, and they shouldn't just go into these realms; they should be sent. They should be sent with the spirit of your family. Much like the Holy Spirit is the ambassador of heaven, your spouse and children should be sent with the mind-set that they are representing your family, and they carry your family name. Your family name has great power and significance. When your spouse leaves for work, or your children leave for school, bless them and send them. The spirit of your family sends them with the understanding that they represent something bigger than themselves. It is family that breaks off the independent mind-set, and it is family that sends them with a sense of belonging and purpose.

For too long, the body of Christ and families in general have been intimidated by the realms of influence. We are fearful of being contaminated by the world or being accused of being manipulative. To subdue the earth, families will need to have the understanding and the awakening that they are the very key to cultural transformation. In order to bring the transformation in which we all are interested, we will have to understand that it is up to us; we are the *critical mass.* We have the Holy Spirit within us, and we have the cultural mandate—it is expected of us to use our gifts and authority, to move out of our comfort zone, and to impact society.

For reasons I can't explain, Christian families have bought into the notion that there is a separation of church and state. To be very clear, the separation of church and state is not in the US Constitution. There is a freedom of religion clause, but that is to keep the government out of religious practices, not to keep Christian influence out of society. We live in a great nation, where anyone can be free to bring influence. We have often confused influence with manipulation, but Christian families have absolutely no need for manipulation. We represent God's perfect plan for society. We simply need to "be family" and not be afraid to enter all aspects of society and shine our light. Our light of influence doesn't need to be sold, promoted, or manipulated. It just needs to be light. The world, whether it realizes it or not, is desperate for light. Our families need to be that light.

# The Light of the World

You are the salt of the earth but if the salt loses
its flavor how shall it be seasoned? It is then good
for nothing but to be thrown out and trampled
underfoot by men. You are the light of the world.
A city that is set on a hill cannot be hidden. Nor do
they light a lamp and put it under a basket, but on
a lamp stand, and it gives light to all who are in the
house. Let your light so shine before men, that they
may see your good works and glorify your Father in
heaven. (Matthew 5:13–16)

As mentioned in the previous chapter, families have an
inheritance that allows vertical growth. Families become the
city upon a hill that is a light that can be easily seen. We need
to understand that it is His light that shines through us, not
our works or our striving. We simply need to shine. But if
our light is hidden within our homes only or placed under a
basket, it has no influence. We need to either bring people
into our homes who can see the light on the lamp stand, or
we need to send our families into society to be a city on a hill
that cannot be hidden.

Your family has influence. Your family is not responsible
for *all* of the pillars of society. Your family is not responsible to
subdue the *whole* earth. Your family has been placed here with
a specific task and purpose to bring influence to the areas of
society that you have been asked to influence. I would exhort
you to begin asking Daddy God what it is that your family is

supposed to carry. What are you supposed to subdue? What is supposed to be under your feet? Each individual nuclear family needs to carry and release culture. *We aren't supposed to be influenced by culture; we are supposed to set the culture.*

# Purposeful Family Culture

The Kingdom of God is made up of the kingdom of heaven and the kingdom of the world. We are to demonstrate the kingdom of heaven and restore and influence the kingdom of the World

To truly bring influence on the earth, we need to have an identity as a family in addition to our identity as sons and daughters. Every home has a family culture. The definition of culture is, "the sum total ways of living, built up by a group of human beings and transmitted from one generation to another." The definition of purpose is, "the reason for which something is done or created or for which something exists."

For something to be purposeful, we must know the reason why we do things and then walk intentionally in everything we do. Therefore, the definition of purposeful family culture is, "The intentional ways of living that are built up by a family and transmitted from one generation to another." Only the heavenly Father can instruct you on what your family culture is to be. I am confident that if you ask Him, He will tell you. A purposeful family culture will take shape as we listen to the dreams that heaven is releasing over our families.

It will take further shape when we speak out loud in front of our children the dreams and the desires that are on our hearts. It is impossible to underestimate the importance of telling stories. Relate to your children the dreams and aspirations and the prophetic words that been spoken over your life. The influence in your family will grow exponentially as your children take these dreams as an inheritance.

It said in Genesis that Esau was a skillful hunter, a man of the field, but Jacob was a mild man, dwelling in tents. The Lord revealed to me that Jacob would listen to the family stories in the tents, and he was activated and inspired by all that was promised to his family. He heard the stories of Abraham and Sarah, Abraham's willingness to sacrifice Isaac, the story of Isaac meeting Rebecca, and most significantly, the promises to Abraham and to his descendants. I can see Jacob sitting at the feet of the storytellers, wide-eyed and mesmerized. A nation was birthed in Jacob's heart before he ever saw it come to pass. Esau was a doer. Jacob was a listener.

Parents need to talk in front of their children. They need to tell them what's on their hearts. They need to tell them their dreams and their family stories. The destiny of your family will be birthed in their hearts, even before they see it with their eyes.

Your family is unlike any other in the world. All Christian families may have similar ingredients but different purposes. Proverbs 29:18 says, "Where there is no vision the people perish." You need to ask the Father what is the vision for *your* family. Every family is different and unique. I don't want your family to look like my family.

We also need to break the myth that for your family to have influence, it needs to be active in formal ministry. I want to remind you that for a season, our family culture was board games. Only the Father knows what the purpose, destiny, and culture your family is to have and in what season. The very first piece of revelation that the Lord gave me in regard to family was that when I played football with my children, it was kingdom. It allowed our family light to shine a little brighter.

One fall, our family vacationed at a resort in northern Minnesota. When I was out playing football with my kids in the field, it began to rain, but it didn't stop us as we enjoyed the game and each other. When we returned to the resort, a housekeeper approached us. With tears in her eyes, she explained how she was moved to see a family enjoying each other so much. She also specifically exhorted me that it was so wonderful to see a father who was willing to play with his children in the rain. She said that when she was growing up, she did not have that experience of family. We were able to encourage and strengthen her, and our simple game of football brought an unexpected influence.

I want to be crystal clear that perhaps the most powerful, influential position on the face of the earth is that of a mother and a father. I am determined to break the mind-set and culture where women say, "I am *just* a stay-at-home mom." Our current society and culture sees it as a second-class calling and that women are not realizing their full potential. I believe with all my heart that it is a crafty lie of the Enemy. The enemy also operates in influence, and he knows that family is the means to the restoration of the world. He will do everything to promote fatherlessness and to make mothers feel unsatisfied and unfulfilled in the raising of their children.

*A man and woman are never more powerful than when they are sowing into and creating a loving culture at home.*

I understand our current economic times, and there is certainly grace for those families that require two incomes, but please understand, there is no higher calling than investing everything you have into your marriage and children and into their inheritance. The return on that investment is bigger than you could possibly imagine. I know this, because this was His idea!

There will be some whom the Father will ask to stay single, and there may be some who are unable or who do not feel led at this time to have children, but they still need to live life in the context of a family. They, of course, are not unqualified or exempt from influence, but I feel they should still be sent and still operate in the context of purposeful family culture.

# The Ingredients of Influence

If all Christian families have similar ingredients but different purposes, then what are some of the similar ingredients? The similar ingredients should be what we found in Genesis 2. In review, this is what the loving Father created for His children when He operated in perfect relationship and presence with His creation. It was a place of life, boundaries, provision, rules and authority, truth, purpose, covenant, freedom, and joy, all rooted in relationship and presence with the almighty Father. This is not an all-inclusive list, but it certainly gives us a picture of the characteristics of a loving home and should be similar ingredients in all Christian homes. While these are wonderful and immensely valuable in the home, how do these characteristics have influence outside of the home?

There is not one day in my clinic practice that I do not deal with the effects and problems of depression, anxiety, and fear. The obvious product of hopelessness is anxiety and fear. So much of what I do as a family physician is reassurance. There is an immense longing and yearning for *peace and joy*. When your home operates with words of life and honor and when your kids can be kids with joyous freedom within loving boundaries, your home will be the most infectious home in the neighborhood. Most parents would love their home to be "the house" where all the kids gather. Make no mistake about it; it won't be the stocked refrigerator or access to video games that draws them to your house. It will be the spirit of joy and peace that is present in your home that will, even for a time, lift some of the oppression that is on their young lives. Peace and joy in your home and in your personal life will be one of the strongest magnets of influence that you can possess in our society today. Be purposeful to speak words of life and encouragement, not only to your kids but to their peers and to all your realms of influence.

The hallmark of living in covenant and receiving covenant promises for your family is peace. This is true, because God formed covenant with His people to demonstrate that He is trustworthy and everlasting. All of His promises are true; God cannot lie.

Hebrews 6:13 says, "For when God made a promise to Abraham, because He could swear by no one greater, He swore by Himself ..."

This oath of promise is still for us today, now under the new covenant, in the blood of Jesus. The terms of the covenant are "all that He has is ours, and all that we have is His." Because this is true, what is demonstrated through covenant people is true peace. True (shalom) peace will always be desired by the world.

*Authenticity and truth* is an important component; not only of your home but in what is conveyed outside of the home. It is critically important for Christian families to look the same at home, at church, and in the world. Our children and other children are closely watching us to see if we are genuine. One of the greatest tools of influence is that of a truly transformed life. The world and especially children are investigating and examining the Christian to see if the blood of Jesus really brings true, verifiable, and authentic transformation. *They are not looking to see if we are perfect; they are looking to see if we are authentic.* If we have different lives at home, at church, and when we are out with our friends, then we are just playing roles; we are actors (hypocrites), and our influence is lost.

If our home operates with rules and authority, purpose, and task, and with boundaries, then we can have great influence outside of our family in respect to how we honor these. *Honor* is a word that unfortunately has lost a lot of meaning in our society. This is mostly true because we have lost our honor and respect for authority. It is hard to operate in the realm of honor when we are insistent on keeping our independent mind-set. When my children listen to me and hear my voice, I do not want them to do this from a place of blind obedience but because of their honor for me as their father. It is through honor, through my children recognizing the place of authority that I have in their lives, that they find pleasure in obeying me.

Obedience is not only implicit in the cultural mandate, but children also need to appreciate their position as children. They need to understand that when they yield to the authority of their parents, they are opening the door for them to receive everything that belongs to them through inheritance. Obedience is not just a biblical commandment; it creates a culture of honor that impacts their family and all of society.

Ephesians 6:1–3 says, "Children obey your parents in the Lord, for this is right. Honor your father and mother, which is the first commandment with promise: that it may be well with you and you may live long on the earth."

Obedience is in place to protect family and to provide the promise of long life. Some commentators, however, have noted the fact that the phrase promising longevity in the Torah is mostly written in plural. This suggests that it may refer to society at large. According to this understanding, the promises emphasizing the crucial importance of a loving, respectful relationship of children toward parents is critical for the ongoing survival and health of society as a whole.

We have been given purpose and task, and there is great influence when we honor our assignments. Within a family structure, the role of parent and the role of children are different, but both are very important. We need to create a culture in our homes where the assignment of being a mother and father is honored and where children honor and are honored in the assignment of being children. Our world today is in desperate need of a vision where families honor one another. Families that honor and respect each other, in action and in word, may be one of the greatest tools and the brightest lights we can bring our society and culture. The world needs to know it's possible.

I would argue that no one does this better than my wife. Amy not only has value for creating a purposeful family culture, but she honors her role as a mother. As a mother of eight children, she obviously gets many comments in regard to the enormity of the task. We are always amazed at how forward and blunt people can be with their comments, even right in front of our children. First, people ask if all of these children are ours. (One woman even asked my wife if all of these children were her "biological" children!) This question is usually followed by some negative affirmation, such as, "I have enough problems just raising my two children. I can't imagine what it must be like having eight!" My wife has never allowed—nor will she ever allow—that statement to stand. Amy always responds with a smile and with a slightly raised volume in her voice, so all our children can hear, as she says, "It is an absolute joy. I wouldn't trade it for the world," or "My children are a delight, and it is my pleasure being their mama!" This is a statement of honor toward her children and a statement of influence toward this inquisitive onlooker.

We need to talk about our coworkers, our pastor, and our president with honor. There will be great transformation in the workplace when we express thankfulness to our boss or manager for our job.

I believe, in many respects, the family and the church have lost influence because we shout about what we don't believe. We are often not charitable and not fair. We sometimes have an angry countenance and too often, we display disunity and in-fighting. Simply put, we do not demonstrate the superior way. This behavior, in turn, results in very little influence in the platforms of government and society, and then we become upset when we are not heard. We do not operate in honor.

Honor, however, does not mean agreement. As Christians in the Father's kingdom, we need a greater understanding of honoring those with whom we disagree. We need to approach our societal problems with the weapon of honor, rather than anger, rumor, or slander. Once again, our goal is influence. Our battle is never against flesh and blood but principalities and powers (Ephesians 6:12), so we can be angry and militant toward the Enemy and his influences, but we need to approach God's children with respect and honor. The doors of influence will swing open, even to those with whom we blatantly disagree, if we care for their hearts rather than just their positions.

I care for a patient who is ideologically much different than I am. I am certain that prior to choosing me as his physician, he read my bio, which is overtly Christian, and knew about my convictions. From the first day I began caring for him, I have shown him the honor and respect that I would give any of my patients. Despite his lifestyle and convictions, I have looked him in the eye and shown him compassion. After I had cared for him for over a year, he shared with me some problems he had with other physicians, many of whom made condescending remarks and had judgmental attitudes. He said it wasn't even what they said but the look in their eyes. He said that I never had "that look" in my eye, and so he could trust me. I am certain that we would disagree on many issues in life, but through honor, I have gained influence and a friend.

The Father, the Son, and the Holy Spirit are unified from everlasting to everlasting. Their family covenant began before the world was even created. It is their *family unity* that is a demonstration for all the families in the world. It is the nuclear family—the structure and bond that is formed between parents and children—that is to be the demonstration of unity on the earth. Paul uses the unity of marriage to describe and explain how Jesus (bridegroom) and the body of Christ (bride) were to operate (Ephesians 5:22–33). If families are to operate toward purpose and task, with purposeful family culture, there needs to be a demonstration of unity in regard to that task and purpose within the family. When the family operates in unity, this too will be a demonstration of power and influence toward the world.

Jesus longed for His people to operate in unity. In John 17:20–22 it says, "I do not pray for these alone, but also for those who will believe in Me through their word; that they all may be one, as you Father, are in Me, and I in You; that they also may be one in Us, that the world may believe that You sent Me. And the glory which you gave Me I have given them, that they *may be one just as We are One ...*" (italics added).

Continuing, in John 17:26 it says, "and I have declared to them Your name, and will declare it, that the love with which You loved me may be in them and I in them."

No one would argue the benefits and the merits of unity. Much more can be accomplished and in greater efficiency when we operate in unity. I believe there is no greater demonstration on the earth of that type of unity than the nuclear family. As stated in these Bible verses, when there is unity, we operate like the family of heaven, and this releases love in the purest form.

If family is nuclear, it will have tremendous influence, either positively or negatively. If family operates outside of unity—if there is no peace and a lack of honor—then the nuclear family is the greatest weapon of mass destruction known to man. When the nuclear family is authentic, unified, peaceful, and honoring, it is the greatest weapon of "mass affection." Family needs to be the greatest demonstration of *love and compassion* on the earth, first inwardly and then outwardly. It is through this influence that families once again will rise up to be all they were created to be. This is how we subdue the earth. It is strong families, demonstrating the heavenly family, rooted in love.

Christian families need to look different. All Christian families should demonstrate to the world that we have a superior way—a superior God. *Influence is birthed out of others seeing what you have, seeing what you offer, and wanting it for themselves.*

The central reason why the garden of Eden worked was relationship and presence with the Father. It always comes back to His presence and our identity. When we operate in the authority of our identity as sons and daughters, we once again get the picture that we are to make the rest of the world look like the garden. The original cultural mandate has not changed. We are responsible to pick it up again and to bring the influence of His love throughout the earth. We, as families, need to be the demonstration of His restorative presence.

I am a son of the Most High God. Because of this, my family has authority, inheritance, and influence. In one generation, everything can shift, and families will have the power restored to subdue the earth!

The next and final chapter of this book is a call for Christian families to take their place in history. You will discover how families will usher in and sustain the restoration of all things and why the time to do so is now.

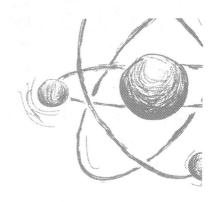

# Chapter 8: Sustainable Energy

## The Time of Family-Led Restoration

My hope and prayer is that by this point in the book, you are fully motivated and inspired to pursue everything that is for your family. I hope that you feel brave and courageous toward restoring all the relationships in your family. It is vitally important to your personal restoration, your family restoration, and the restoration of the world. This raises two final questions: First, are Christian families and the church ready for this message? Second, is the power to subdue the earth through families sustainable?

To find the answer to the first question, we need to go back to the beginning of families and to the beginning of the church, to find their original mandates.

Returning to the culture and the environment of the garden, we once again find the heavenly family creating an earthly family in their image. The Lord gives them the dominion and authority in the first Great Commission to be fruitful, multiply, and fill the earth and subdue it. They were to be in the very presence of the almighty Father, listen to His instruction, and fulfill the tasks they were given.

Because they were in relationship and presence, Adam, Eve, and their children would operate in perfect unity, hearing one voice, and would begin the task of making the rest of the earth look like the garden. Their relationships with each other and with creation would be pure in motivation and honor.

It was when sin entered the garden that we were separated from the presence of our loving Father. We became orphans, and what used to operate in unity now operated in enmity. Again, it was this very orphan spirit that fueled the enmity between relationships and all of mankind.

As soon as man fell, the loving Father set His plan into motion to bring restoration. The seed of the woman (the very woman who allowed sin into the garden) would be the One to bring the restoration of all things. It was a beautiful demonstration of a loving Father who was all about relationship.

Jesus was the family restoration project; His blood was sufficient. He took our enmity, and it was nailed to the cross. He destroyed enmity, and He destroyed the works of the Evil One but, interestingly, He did not destroy the Evil One. Remember, Satan was in the garden, but he was of no effect. He did not have rule, reign, or any authority. Adam and Eve had the authority, and they were to have dominion and to subdue Satan, just as with the rest of creation.

So when Jesus brought restoration to the world through His death and resurrection, He once again rendered the Enemy powerless. I believe He restored the original conditions of the garden and, most important, our relationship with the Father. We might have loved it if Jesus had just removed the Enemy altogether, but instead, Jesus restored the authority structure here on earth through the power of His name, so that while the Satan is still present, the enemy is once again of no effect. The Father once again trusts us with His creation, and we once again need to rule in the presence of our enemies.

# Back at the Beginning

So here we are, back at the beginning. The Father has placed us on the earth in His image. He has restored our dominion and authority as sons and daughters of the Most High God. We have restored relationship, and we get to enjoy His presence. The earth is still unsubdued, and we have been given the mandate to subdue it. The Enemy is still present, but he is of no effect, unless, once again, we give our authority to him.

Compared to Adam and Eve, we have a few advantages and a few disadvantages. We have the advantage of the teachings, the death, the resurrection, and the blood of Jesus. We have Scripture as a guide. We have the major advantage of not only having God with us but God in us. We have the advantage of knowing more about our Enemy and his certain future.

We have the disadvantage in that not all of the earth is under the blood of Jesus. Many of the people today have still surrendered their authority to the Father of Lies. The unfortunate effects and devastation of sin is still rampant all over the world. God's people and God's families need to have courage and strength to be a light in the midst of darkness.

We, as families in the new covenant and as the New Testament church, need to understand our place in history and fully receive the impact of every drop of blood that Jesus shed for us, so that we can live a victorious, powerful, and effective life for His kingdom. My concern, however, is that Christians today aren't living kingdom-minded but rather are living with an Old Testament mind-set.

Those who lived during the Old Testament times relied on Scripture and the prophets of old. With hope, they would appropriately look toward the coming of the Messiah. They lived out of reach of true salvation, confirmed by their oppressive conditions. They would cry out to heaven, "How much longer will you make us wait, Lord, until we will behold our salvation?"

Now, we live on the other side of the cross and have received our salvation. Instead of fully embracing the restorative power of Jesus' blood, all we do is dance at the door and continue to lament in our oppression. We still cry out to heaven, "How much longer will you make us wait, Lord, until you send Jesus back to us and remove us from this place?"

The second coming of Jesus is truly our "blessed hope," and I would never seek to minimize the importance of His return. When Jesus returns, however, it will *not* be as a Savior; it will be as a Bridegroom! We already have been saved and rescued, and now we are called to be His bride. He is returning with fire in His eyes as a Bridegroom for His bride. We are no longer under the spirit of bondage but under the Spirit of His Son.

# The Revealing of the Sons of God

For you did not receive the spirit of bondage again to fear, but you received the Spirit of adoption by whom we cry out, "Abba, Father." The Spirit himself bears witness with our spirit that we are children of God, and if children, then heirs—heirs of God and joint heirs with Christ, if indeed we suffer with Him that we may also be glorified together. For I consider that the sufferings of this present time are not worthy to be compared with the glory which shall be revealed in us. For the earnest expectation of the creation eagerly waits for the revealing of the sons of God. For the creation was subjected to futility, not willingly, but because of Him who subjected it in hope; because the creation itself also will be delivered from the bondage of corruption into the glorious liberty of the children of God. For we know that the whole creation groans and labors with birth pangs together until *now*. (Romans 8:15–21, italics added)

We have already learned so much from this passage. We learned that the spirit of bondage and the spirit of fear are defeated when we understand our position as children of God. We learned that since we are children, we have inheritance.

Furthermore, we learned that creation itself was subjected to bondage and now, just like in the garden, we, as children, are to exercise our dominion and liberate creation. This is accomplished by sons and daughters being revealed on the earth and taking back their rightful authority and entering every aspect of society to release His freedom. This is influencing and subduing the earth. Creation and culture will be transformed when it is exposed to the glory that is revealed in us. *Creation is waiting for us!* It has been waiting for us since the moment Jesus rose from the dead. I believe creation still groans for us, and the time for the revealing of the sons of God is now.

The Father is in a partying mood, His Son is crazy in love with us, and even creation itself is waiting for us. This is no time to curl up in the fetal position. There is work to be done, and the time is now. We need to understand that there is no plan B, only plan A. It is up to our families to fulfill the original mandate.

I believe Christian families today are very ready for this message. I believe there is a longing for this message. The nuclear family has lost its luster; it has lost its purpose; it has forgotten why it was created. I hope this will be a clarion call to all families to be all they were created to be.

# The Times of Restoration

I also feel that the church today needs to be ready to receive, equip, and send healthy families, full of influence, into the world to get the job done. I believe the early church had a vision for this and operated in the power necessary to achieve the task. Peter explained this very well in Acts 3. The picture of how this story took place is critical to the understanding of Peter's message. Peter and John went to the temple to pray. They saw a lame man at the gate called Beautiful. This man was familiar to the crowd because he was placed there daily to ask for alms.

Peter said to him, "Silver and gold I do not have, but what I do have I give you: in the name of Jesus Christ of Nazareth, rise up and walk."

The man was instantly restored and began leaping and praising God. The people were amazed, and the commotion from the healed man attracted a crowd. As they entered the temple, the healed man followed them, holding onto Peter and John.

Picture Peter addressing the crowd, while this joyous man, who was just restored, held onto him and clutched him.

> Men of Israel, why do you marvel at this? Or why look so intently at us, as though by our own power or godliness we made this man walk? The God of Abraham, Isaac, and Jacob, the God of our fathers, glorified His servant Jesus, whom you delivered up and denied in the presence of Pilate, when he was determined to let him go. But you denied the Holy One and the Just and asked for a murderer to be granted to you, and killed the Prince of life whom God raised from the dead, of which we are witnesses. And His name, through faith in His name, has made this man strong, whom you see and know. Yes, the faith which comes through Him has given him this *perfect soundness* in the presence of you all. Yet now, brethren, I know that you did

it in ignorance, as did also your rulers. But those things which God foretold by the mouth of all His prophets, that the Christ would suffer, He has thus fulfilled. Repent therefore and be converted, that your sins may be blotted out, so that times of refreshing may come from the *presence* of the Lord, and that He may send Jesus Christ who was preached to you before, whom heaven must receive until *the times of restoration of all things*, which God has spoken by the mouth of all His holy prophets since the world began. For Moses truly said to the fathers, the Lord your God will raise up for you a prophet like me from your brethren. Him you shall hear in all things, whatever He says to you. And it shall be that every soul who will not hear that prophet shall be utterly destroyed from among the people. Yes, and all the prophets, from Samuel and those who follow as many as have spoken, have also foretold *these days*. You are sons of the prophets, and of the covenant which God made with our fathers saying to Abraham, and in your seed *all the families of the earth* shall be blessed. (Acts 3:12–25, italics added)

I believe this is an incredibly profound and important historical dissertation. The early church understood the times in which they lived. They were ready for this message, and it should be an inspiration for us today.

First, there is physical healing. Another word for perfect soundness is restoration. Peter asked why they would even marvel at this, because in his view, restoration would be the normal, natural result of the life, death, and resurrection of Jesus Christ.

Second, the prophets foretold that faith in the name of Jesus would not only result in the restoration of this lame man but also usher in "the times of restoration of *all* things." We are the sons of the prophets. We are His covenant people. As a result, we live in a special time. There is no way an argument could be made—based on the context and the use of present tense throughout the passage, as well as in the setting of a man miraculously restored—that the time of restoration of all things is in the future. Peter made it clear that the time everybody had been waiting for is now.

Third, we learn that the manifestation and confirmation that this special time has come is the restored presence of the Lord (where we find our refreshment), miracles and healing (as they just witnessed), and families of the earth being blessed (yeah!).

The remainder of the book of Acts is filled with story after story of exactly what Peter predicted would manifest. As soon as Jesus rose from the dead and commissioned us with His authority, it was the start of the times of restoration of all things. Somewhere along the annals of time, however, many have lost the new covenant picture. They have unfortunately placed themselves back under the spirit of bondage, where there is no relationship, purpose, or power. The church cannot turn its gaze to sometime in the future; there is too much to be done now.

Jesus loves His bride and wants her to walk in the fullness of her destiny. He wants her to be pure, spotless, and without wrinkle. He also desperately loves all of those who don't yet call upon His name. The second Great Commission, which builds upon the first Great Commission, tells us to teach the world about Jesus. Families need to lead the way. They need to enter churches already restored, so they can be trained and equipped, and so they can be the bride that participates in the times of restoration of all things. The second Great Commission cannot be accomplished without the first.

No one knows when Jesus will return, and I don't know the full mystery and drama of the book of Revelation. I understand that there is real evil and a battle. I look forward to another "fullness of time" moment when Jesus will return, and we will behold Him face-to-face. However, if you lined up one hundred theologians and asked them to explain the book of Revelation, you most likely would get one hundred different answers—there seems to be confusion. Where the rest of Scripture seems to operate in clarity, the book of Revelation seems to be cloudy and opaque. I feel the confusion is not the problem; rather, it is the point. The Father doesn't want us to focus on the end but on the task at hand. He certainly wants us to operate in wisdom and discernment in the end times, and I feel He will bring further clarity as the times draw nearer, but our focus now needs to be on His eyes, His words, and the tasks He has for us to do. I feel there is still work to be done. My family and I want to fully participate in that work.

The church needs to be ready for this message. It is time for the body of Christ to once again catch the culture of the church in the book of Acts. It is time for the church to operate in the miraculous, and not see it as supernatural, but as the natural result and outflow of the work of Jesus. Also, it should not just be an occasional experience in a church setting but should be commonplace and common culture in every Christian home. The church needs to realize that the time is now.

As Peter explained and the prophets foretold, it is our covenant promise that in the "times of restoration of all things," every family will be blessed. This makes perfect sense, because family should be on the front line of this movement. If families and churches position themselves, if they catch this vision, they will contribute to the greatest restoration and transformation the world has ever seen.

# The Garden Template

If we do catch the vision for the importance of family restoration and the vision for family as the means of restoration of the world, how will we know if it is sustainable?

History tells us that the first church found in the book of Acts was clearly not sustained. History also tells us that there have been many revivals and awakenings that brought great transformation and rapid cultural change. These, too, seemed to be ignited for a generation and then would taper off and die. It doesn't seem like this template would be God's best plan.

God's best plan is, once again, found in the garden. If you haven't figured this out already, the template God used to spread and reproduce His culture all over the earth was family. In my opinion, the reason this movement of God will be sustainable, unlike other revivals, is that it is based on the original mandate and template, set up from the beginning of time.

We must never forget that it is God who is constant and invariable. So if revivals come and go, it is not based on the movements of God but on the ability or inability of man to steward God's presence. In the book of Acts or in historical revivals and awakenings, the presence of God was stewarded by a single person or group of people who recognized and hosted His presence. The flame would burn as long as these people were alive, present, or had the fortitude to sustain it. Most often, the problem was that it was not reproduced. The next generation was not trained in how to handle the flame, or they had no value for it.

*In the garden, however, families were set into place to not only hold and sustain the culture but to reproduce it.* The template in the garden was to be fruitful in order to multiply, to multiply in order to fill the earth, and to fill the earth in order to subdue it. When the rest of the earth would look like the garden, with the sustaining presence of the loving Father, there would be no need for revivals. The value for the presence of the Lord would be inherent and would easily be passed from generation to generation.

This is why I am so excited about the notion of family-led restoration. In my opinion, we need restoration, not revival. We need to be restored, not awakened. Please don't misunderstand me; I am appreciative and stirred by any manifestation of the presence of the Lord at any time, in any environment. It is in the presence and the glory of the Lord that brings about real change. To subdue the earth, however, requires that families have a sustaining, generational mind-set. Families must steward the presence and then teach their children to steward and value the presence. This is the template; this will work because this is what God originally intended.

Historically, the families of the revivalists would often suffer. The revivalist leader often would be overwhelmed by the intoxication or would feel the burden of hosting the presence. This responsibility, at times, would result in the abandonment of the family. I am confident that this is not what the Lord intended. Family-led restoration may not have "glory cloud"-type experiences at first, but it does create the sustainable environment for the "glory cloud" to come *and* to stay. This can then be passed on to generations that listen to Daddy's voice and value His presence. It is easy to see how this culture could quickly and effectively change the world.

Simply put, the power to subdue the earth is not sustainable without strong nuclear families.

# One Language, One Mandate

The notion for the "restoration of all things" is not far-fetched or unsustainable. It is at the very heart of the all-knowing, all-loving, all-powerful God. This God made a covenant with you and your family from the beginning of time, and He swore by His name and by His Son's blood that what He has promised will come to pass. Nothing is impossible through an almighty God. The blood that flowed through Jesus' veins was the blood of restoration. All I know is that God the Father sent His Son to die for me. Anything that happens after that, anything that is the result of that blood, is not far-fetched.

We can learn a lot from an unlikely story in the book of Genesis. The Tower of Babel occurred only several generations after Noah and his sons. As previously described, these generations were most likely very intelligent and very capable. I have explained throughout this book that the cultural mandate didn't end. What God put into place and spoke into being was set. Throughout the book of Genesis, God's mandate to be fruitful, multiply, and fill the earth was often reiterated, although rarely followed.

The story is told in Genesis 11:1–6.

> Now the whole earth had one language and one speech. And it came to pass, as they journeyed from the east, that they found a plain in the land of Shinar, and they dwelt there. Then they said to one another, "Come let us make bricks and bake them thoroughly." They had brick for stone, and they had asphalt for mortar. And they said, "Come let us build ourselves a city, and a tower whose top is in the heavens; let us make a name for ourselves, lest we be scattered abroad over the face of the whole earth." But the Lord came down to see the city and the tower which the sons of men had built. And the Lord said, indeed the people are one and they all have one language, and this is what they begin to do; now *nothing they propose to do will be withheld from them.* (Italics added)

Sin did not remove the cultural mandate. Sin, however, did separate the people alive during the tower of Babel from the voice of the Father. They still had the resource and capability to subdue the earth, except for the most important element—His presence. Because they were not listening to the Father's voice, they operated outside of His perfect plan. They disobeyed the mandate to fill the earth; instead, they gathered together. They operated with an independent spirit, with the goal of self-exultation. They could accomplish great things through the unity of one language, but it was not heaven's language.

Out of compassion, God confused their language and scattered them. He knew they were orphans, and they weren't listening to His voice. If they weren't listening to His voice, they would definitely listen to another voice that would ultimately lead to their certain destruction.

Despite their rebellion and distortion, the Father Himself recognized their amazing capability through the power of their unity, saying, "Now nothing they propose to do will be withheld from them." Considering their situation and their rebellion, this is a staggering statement, but it should give us great hope for our families in the world today.

Today, we have been given the hope of restoration. He has given us the means toward sustainable restoration— that is, the nuclear family. He has given us the power for restoration—that is, the authority through Jesus' blood and the abiding presence of the Holy Spirit. Once again, He has given us His voice. We are no longer separated. While orphans may hear many voices, sons and daughters only hear their Daddy's voice. We can once again operate in perfect unity, as we all speak the same language—heaven's language. We don't operate in rebellion; we operate in the center of His plan—His mandate. Considering our situation, I am confident in saying, "Now nothing we propose to do will be withheld from us."

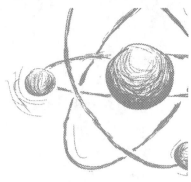

# Conclusion

Before you begin a restoration project, you need to know its inherent value and what it originally looked like. I hope this book satisfied both of those requirements. In conclusion, however, you need to ask yourself one more important question: "Is it worth it?" Pursuing restoration most likely requires a large investment, perseverance, and emotional pain. Is it worth it?

To Christians: *it is worth it!* You, as followers of Christ, need to stop dancing at the door, enter the Father's kingdom, and begin the adventure. You need to fully understand that you are sons and daughters of the Most High God. When you first understand your position, you can allow the overwhelming love of the Father to displace any orphan issues that are within you. Don't move past identity. You can then be completely satisfied and fulfilled in the presence of your Daddy and not have to look to others to meet your needs. If you steward your identity, it will begin the process of healing your family relationships and securing your authority and inheritance.

To marriages: *it is worth it!* It is never too late. With identities secured, your marriage can once again operate as "one flesh." Christian marriages need to look different. They are built on covenant and are everlasting. The best way to defend true marriage is to display true marriage. Your marriage is too pure and too important to be in disrepair or to be ineffective or redefined.

To parents: *it is worth it!* It is time to honor the assignment. You have everything you need for your children, and you are fully equipped. You have the opportunity every day to display the love of the Father to your children. You are the culture-setter and the keeper of your home. You get to speak life, create boundaries, and create a culture of peace and joy over your home and your children. No one else can do your job; you are fully able.

To children: *it is worth it!* It is time for you to honor the assignment. You get to obey and honor your parents, which will unlock a double portion. You need to value your birthright. You have a tremendous opportunity to sit at your parents' feet and receive everything from them as an inheritance. You live in the security and in the unity of a family. Treasure and steward that position.

To families: *it is worth it!* You have been given a mandate from the beginning of time. Be fruitful and multiply, fill the earth, and subdue it. This mandate is still available to you today. The Father is asking for your family to fulfill its destiny. Anything that you can do to strengthen your family and bring restoration is central to His plan. This mission is not for the weakhearted, but you not only have each other; you have the backing of all of heaven.

Outside of the Trinity, no one has done family perfectly. The message in this book needs to propel us forward, not have us sit in regret. Time is too short for condemnation. We need to feel the urgency and the importance of the time in which we live. There is hope! I believe the restoration of family needs to break out all over the world, and the time is now. It starts with identity, and it ends with the restoration of all things.

Now is the time for *your* family to be powerful. It is time for your family to be restored and to subdue the earth, and I promise you this: it will be worth it.

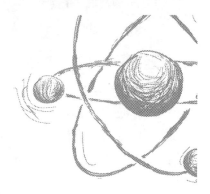

# Sources

Benner, Jeff A. "Subdue?" *Ancient Hebrew Research Center Biblical E- Magazine*, issue # 027, May, 2006 *www.ancient-hebrew.org.*

Carter, Joe. "Be Fruitful. Multiply." *Comment Magazine* November 5, 2010. *www.cardus.ca.*

Chapman, Gary. *The Five Love Languages: How to Express Heartfelt Commitment to Your Mate.* Chicago, Illinois: Northfield Publishing, 1995.

Claussen, Heather. *Stepping Stones: God's Covenant Plan through the Ages.* Bloomington, IN: WestBow Press, 2014.

Isaac, Ashok. "Sons are Free: Healing the Orphan Heart." May 4, 2012. *www.sure-mercies.net.*

Rosen, David. "The Family in Judaism: Past, Present and Future, Fears and Hopes." *www.rabbidavidrosen.net.*

Waters, Vikki. "Healing the Heart of the Family." 2009. *www.iggm.org.*

Wolters, Albert. *The Foundational Command: "Subdue the Earth!"* Toronto, Ontario: Institute for Christian Studies, 1973.

Yeulett, Paul. "One Flesh-The Profound Mystery." October 3, 2008 *www.banneroftruth.org.*

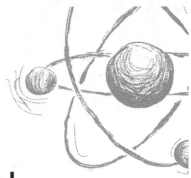

# About the Author

Dr. Jonathan Claussen is a family practitioner in Staples, Minnesota. He is married to his beloved wife, Amy, and is raising eight fabulous children. His family hosts regional worship and revival meetings in their home, known as the Glory Barn.

Dr. Claussen is also the founder and president of the Family Restoration Project. It was created to bring restoration, first of all, to our identity in the Father, as sons and daughters, which then creates strong marriages, empowered parents, and healthy families. Dynamic Christian families, in turn, display the power and influence needed to bring restoration to the entire world.

The Family Restoration Project is led by Jonathan and Amy, their children, and both sets of their parents. They are a family that blesses families. They travel the country and produce vital resources that release their transformational family message. To learn more about the Claussen family or to invite them to your church or ministry, visit www.familyrestorationproject.com.